RUSSELL KIRK'S

CONCISE GUIDE TO CONSERVATISM

INTRODUCTION BY WILFRED M. McCLAY

REGNERY GATEWAY

Regnery Gateway™ is a registered trademark of Salem Communications Holding Corporation

Regnery° is a registered trademark of Salem Communications Holding Corporation

Cataloging-in-Publication data on file with the Library of Congress

ISBN 978-1-62157-878-9
e-book ISBN 978-1-62157-879-6

Published in the United States by
Regnery Publishing
A Division of Salem Media Group
300 New Jersey Ave NW
Washington, DC 20001
www.Regnery.com

Manufactured in the United States of America

10 9 8 7 6 5 4 3 2

Books are available in quantity for promotional or premium use. For information on discounts and terms, please visit our website: www.Regnery.com.

Contents

Introduction   vii

Chapter I
The Essence of Conservatism   1

Chapter II
Conservatives and Religious Faith   9

Chapter III
Conservatives and Conscience   17

Chapter IV
Conservatives and Individuality   25

Chapter V
Conservatives and the Family   33

Chapter VI
Conservatives and the Community   39

Chapter VII
Conservatives and Just Government   45

Chapter VIII
Conservatives and Private Property   53

Chapter IX
Conservatives and Power   63

Chapter X
Conservatives and Education   71

Chapter XI
Permanence and Change   81

Chapter XII
What Is the Republic?   91

Index   105

Introduction

Wilfred M. McClay

Much ink has been spilled and countless pixels set aglow in debates over that elusive thing called "conservatism." In fact, conservatism has been suffering from a deepening identity crisis for some time now, especially in the United States. The candidacy, election, and presidency of Donald Trump have only accelerated a process that began at least three decades ago with the end of the Reagan administration, and probably much earlier than that. No one seems to be able to say with confidence just what "conservatism" means today.

The problem may be unavoidable. Because the United States is an unusually fluid society, valuing liberty more than order and esteeming social mobility as one of our principal virtues, it is often unclear what the word "conservative" means for us—not as clear as it would be if, say, we lived in a relatively static agricultural society governed by stable landed elites with deep roots and well-established customs of social deference. But our society is nothing of the sort. Therefore, those who don the mantle of "conservative" in

America today are an astonishingly diverse lot, ranging from libertarian zealots who embrace the "creative destruction" of unregulated capitalism and the ceaseless reconstruction of social and cultural institutions to traditionalists who look back longingly to the solidarity, reciprocity, and faithful integration of medieval European society. What common ground could there be between such extremes? No wonder that even sympathetic observers find the spectacle of American conservatism bewildering and turn away from it in confusion and dismay.

When asked to define conservatism, Russell Kirk often resorted to an answer formulated by the Harvard intellectual historian H. Stuart Hughes: conservatism is the negation of ideology. That is in fact a very good answer, or at least the beginning of a very good one. But part of the problem today is that so many conservatives in America are in fact ideologues, whether they know it or not. They are much more interested in conserving and extending the career of certain ideological principles than in conserving and perpetuating the complex web of social arrangements and practices that have proved their worth through the generations. And to make matters worse, the principles being conserved are frequently different for different parties. The force of "conservatism," therefore, may be deployed on both sides, "pro" and "con" alike, of a great many issues of public policy: American leadership in the world, free trade, drug legalization, gay marriage, property rights, immigration restriction, civil rights, and so on. Who would be surprised to see an article announcing "the conservative case for euthanasia" or flatly opposing the principle of religious liberty on "conservative" grounds? If such articles haven't been published yet, it's only a matter of time.

But there is nothing inevitable about this state of confusion. In fact, there is a strong basis for a balanced and entirely sensible American conservatism, and Russell Kirk lays it out with admirable clarity in the pages of this sturdy book, whose reissue comes at just the right moment, when we need a recovery and revitalization of conservatism, not as something reinvented but as a body of wisdom that has stood the test of time, resisting precipitous and ideologically motivated change, countering the passions of abstract revolutionizing ideology with the concrete virtue of prudence.

The Kirkian way of communicating ideas is quite different from the sloganeering of the present day, but changes in rhetorical fashion have not diminished its appeal. To those who are accustomed to thinking of conservatism as chiefly a matter of policy wonkery presented in crisp quantitative tables and jargon-laden bureaucratic prose, Kirk's message, with its historical sweep and poetic splendor, its delight in beauty and fancy, its disdain for academicism in all forms, and its talent for making us feel the vital connection between ourselves and the stories of vanished peoples and things of the past, will come as a great and pleasant surprise.

For Kirk, conservatism is not a set of policy desiderata. It is a disposition of grateful wonder at the miracle of our existence, calling us to acknowledge the sources of our being and to strive to live in respectful and loving harmony with them. It is grounded ultimately in Edmund Burke's sweeping vision of the "contract of eternal society," linking the dead, the living, and those yet to be born in a mysterious triple braid of shared joys, obligations, and memories.

One of the many myths about American conservatism is that it is the complacent outlook of the wealthy classes and stands apart from the great American story of individual striving and advancement. But Kirk's origins were themselves humble and quintessentially American. He was born in 1918 in Plymouth, Michigan, to a struggling middle-class family living in a prefabricated house that lacked an indoor bathroom. Nor did he have access to the best educational opportunities. Like so many of the most remarkable Americans, such as Abraham Lincoln and Frederick Douglass, Kirk was able to parlay a voracious love of reading into a superior education with a bit of help from solidly traditional public schools that provided him with scope for his literary and debating skills.

It was not until his postwar graduate studies at the University of St. Andrews that Kirk was fully formed as a conservative thinker. It had everything to do with being in Scotland. The atmosphere, lore, landscape, architecture, and people of that country all enchanted him and quickened his literary pulse. He wrote, among other things, three books, seven short stories, and twenty-five scholarly articles during his four years at St. Andrews, establishing a pattern of astonishing productivity that he would continue for another four decades. The most important of his writings during that time was his doctoral dissertation, which was eventually published in 1953 as *The Conservative Mind*, one of the truly indispensable books in American conservative intellectual history and arguably the most important of all his books.

Of course, 1953 was an *annus mirabilis* for the American conservative mind. In particular, it was an extraordinarily fertile year for conservative books. In addition to Kirk's magnum opus, Robert Nisbet's *Quest for Community*, Leo Strauss's *Natural Right and History*, and Daniel Boorstin's *The Genius of American Politics* were published. And in the years immediately before and after, luminaries such as T. S. Eliot, Ray Bradbury, Christopher Dawson, Eric Voegelin, C. S. Lewis, Whittaker Chambers, William F. Buckley Jr., and Francis Graham Wilson published works of great, and even monumental, importance to conservatives.

But Kirk did something that none of these other authors did. He sought to prove that Anglo-American conservatism was not a recent invention, that it had a usable past, a venerable history of thinkers extending back at least to Edmund Burke, if not a great deal further, and forward to such contemporary figures as George Santayana and Eliot. And as his biographer Brad Birzer has insisted, "in [Kirk's] definition of the conservative, the poetic, literary, and theological superseded the political." As Kirk explained in 1952 to Henry Regnery, the publisher of *The Conservative Mind*, it was imperative to "recognize the great importance, in literature as in life, of religion, ethics, and beauty." Politics, he snapped, "is the diversion of the quarter-educated, and I do try to transcend pure politics in my book."

Not that Kirk ignored politics in his own life; nor would he do so today. But he might well complain, were he with us now, that conservatism has been impoverished in recent years by an overemphasis on ideological forms of politics and the neglect of the realm of the imagination and of the realm of culture more generally, realms in which the conservative sensibility had in the past been powerfully represented. Today we often hear that politics is downstream from culture, an observation that would have seemed obvious to Kirk. It may well be, then, that the transformation of a feckless, life-denying, and inhumane culture into something more consonant with our human endowment is the principal task facing conservatives and conservatism.

To the achievement of that worthy goal, this short book—originally published in 1957 under the title *The Intelligent Woman's Guide to Conservatism*, a gentle gibe at George Bernard Shaw's *Intelligent Woman's Guide to Socialism and Capitalism*—is an unfailingly graceful and pithy contribution. With remarkably direct prose that is effortlessly read, this book is a minor wonder, an introduction to the core of American conservatism, as delightful as it is instructive. Readers who complain about the occasionally antique and florid style of *The Conservative Mind* will be impressed here by the limpid and accessible prose. A highly skilled professional writer, Kirk knew how to write appropriately for whatever occasion or medium presented itself, whether it was an op-ed column or a ghost story or a door-stopping tome. Very few writers can claim as much.

Most amazingly of all, this book has required no dramatic revision after the passage of sixty-two years. That very fact gives it unexpected weight. Kirk's insights about family, the importance of private property, education, religion, and a dozen other subjects not only remain completely sound but now seem downright prophetic. See if you don't agree. If that's not proof that Kirk's conservatism was grounded in the Permanent Things, I don't know what is.

Wilfred M. McClay holds the G. T. and Libby Blankenship Chair in the History of Liberty at the University of Oklahoma and is the director of the Center for the History of Liberty. His most recent book is Land of Hope: An Invitation to the Great American Story *(Encounter, 2019).*

CHAPTER I

The Essence of Conservatism

M odern conservatism took form about the beginning of the French Revolution, when far-seeing men in England and America perceived that if humanity is to conserve the elements in civilization that make life worth living, some coherent body of ideas must resist the leveling and destructive impulse of fanatic revolutionaries. In England, the founder of true conservatism was Edmund Burke, whose *Reflections on the Revolution in France* turned the tide of British opinion and influenced incalculably the leaders of society in the Continent and in America. In the newly established United States, the fathers of the Republic, conservative by training and by practical experience, were determined to shape constitutions which should guide their posterity in enduring ways of justice and freedom. Our American War of Independence had not been a real revolution, but rather a separation from England; statesmen of Massachusetts and Virginia had no desire to turn society upside down. In their writings, especially in the works of John Adams, Alexander Hamilton, and James Madison, we find a sober and tested conservatism founded upon an understanding of history and human nature. The Constitution which the leaders of that generation drew up has proved to be the most successful conservative device in all history.

Conservative leaders, ever since Burke and Adams, have subscribed to certain general ideas that we may set down, briefly, by way of definition. Conservatives distrust what Burke called "abstractions"—that is, absolute political dogmas divorced from practical experience and particular circumstances. They do believe, nevertheless, in the existence of certain abiding truths which govern the conduct of human society. Perhaps the chief principles which have characterized American conservative thought are these:

1. Men and nations are governed by moral laws; and those laws have their origin in a wisdom that is more than human—in divine justice. At heart, political problems are moral and religious problems. The wise statesman tries to apprehend the moral law and govern his conduct accordingly. We have a moral debt to our ancestors, who bestowed upon us our civilization, and a moral obligation to the generations who will come after us. This debt is ordained of God. We have no right, therefore, to tamper impudently with human nature or with the delicate fabric of our civil social order.

2. Variety and diversity are the characteristics of a high civilization. Uniformity and absolute

equality are the death of all real vigor and freedom in existence. Conservatives resist with impartial strength the uniformity of a tyrant or an oligarchy, and the uniformity of what Tocqueville called "democratic despotism."

3. Justice means that every man and every woman have the right to what is their own—to the things best suited to their own nature, to the rewards of their ability and integrity, to their property and their personality. Civilized society requires that all men and women have equal rights before the law, but that equality should not extend to equality of condition: that is, society is a great partnership, in which all have equal rights—but not to equal things. The just society requires sound leadership, different rewards for different abilities, and a sense of respect and duty.

4. Property and freedom are inseparably connected; economic leveling is not economic progress. Conservatives value property for its own sake, of course; but they value it even more because without it all men and women are at the mercy of an omnipotent government.

5. Power is full of danger; therefore, the good state is one in which power is checked and balanced, restricted by sound constitutions and

customs. So far as possible, political power ought to be kept in the hands of private persons and local institutions. Centralization is ordinarily a sign of social decadence.

6. The past is a great storehouse of wisdom; as Burke said, "The individual is foolish, but the species is wise." The conservative believes that we need to guide ourselves by the moral traditions, the social experience, and the whole complex body of knowledge bequeathed to us by our ancestors. The conservative appeals beyond the rash opinion of the hour to what Chesterton called "the democracy of the dead"—that is, the considered opinions of the wise men and women who died before our time, the experience of the race. The conservative, in short, knows he was not born yesterday.

7. Modern society urgently needs true community: and true community is a world away from collectivism. Real community is governed by love and charity, not by compulsion. Through churches, voluntary associations, local governments, and a variety of institutions, conservatives strive to keep community healthy. Conservatives are not selfish, but public-spirited. They know that collectivism means the end of real community, substituting uniformity for variety and force for willing cooperation.

8. In the affairs of nations, the American conservative feels that his country ought to set an example to the world, but ought not to try to remake the world in its image. It is a law of politics, as well as of biology, that every living thing loves above all else—even above its own life—its distinct identity, which sets it off from all other things. The conservative does not aspire to domination of the world, nor does he relish the prospect of a world reduced to a single pattern of government and civilization.

9. Men and women are not perfectible, conservatives know; and neither are political institutions. We cannot make a heaven on earth, though we may make a hell. We all are creatures of mingled good and evil; and, good institutions neglected and ancient moral principles ignored, the evil in us tends to predominate. Therefore, the conservative is suspicious of all utopian schemes. He does not believe that, by power of positive law, we can solve all the problems of humanity. We can hope to make our world tolerable, but we cannot make it perfect. When progress is achieved, it is through prudent recognition of the limitations of human nature.

10. Change and reform, conservatives are convinced, are not identical: moral and political

innovation can be destructive as well as benefi-
cial; and if innovation is undertaken in a spirit
of presumption and enthusiasm, probably it
will be disastrous. All human institutions alter
to some extent from age to age, for slow change
is the means of conserving society, just as it is
the means for renewing the human body. But
American conservatives endeavor to reconcile
the growth and alteration essential to our life
with the strength of our social and moral traditions. With Lord Falkland, they say, "When it
is not necessary to change, it is necessary not
to change." They understand that men and
women are best content when they can feel that
they live in a stable world of enduring values.

In the short chapters which follow, I shall touch upon these
several principles of conservatism, directly or indirectly; and I
shall address also the conservatives' attitude toward religion,
the family, education, and some of the pressing issues of the day.

Conservatism, then, is not simply the concern of the people who have much property and influence; it is not simply the
defense of privilege and status. Most conservatives are neither
rich nor powerful. But they do, even the most humble of them,
derive great benefits from our established Republic. They have
liberty, security of person and home, equal protection of the
laws, the right to the fruits of their industry, and opportunity
to do the best that is in them. They have a right to personality
in life, and a right to consolation in death. Conservative

principles shelter the hopes of everyone in society. And conservatism is a social concept important to everyone who desires equal justice and personal freedom and all the lovable old ways of humanity. Conservatism is not simply a defense of "capitalism." ("Capitalism," indeed, is a word coined by Karl Marx, intended from the beginning to imply that the only thing conservatives defend is vast accumulations of private capital.) But the true conservative does stoutly defend private property and a free economy, both for their own sake and because these are means to great ends.

Those great ends are more than economic and more than political. They involve human dignity, human personality, and human happiness. They involve even the relationship between God and man. For the radical collectivism of our age is fiercely hostile to any other authority: modern radicalism detests religious faith, private virtue, traditional personality, and the life of simple satisfactions. Everything worth conserving is menaced in our generation. Mere unthinking negative opposition to the current of events, clutching in despair at what we still retain, will not suffice in this age. A conservatism of instinct must be reinforced by a conservatism of thought and imagination.

CHAPTER II

Conservatives and Religious Faith

Not all religious people are conservatives; and not all conservatives are religious people. Christianity prescribes no especial form of politics. There have been famous radicals who were devout Christians—though most radicals have been nothing of the sort. All the same, there could be no conservatism without a religious foundation, and it is conservative people, by and large, who defend religion in our time.

Quintin Hogg, a talented English conservative of the twentieth century, in his little book *The Case for Conservatism*, remarks, "There is nothing I despise more than a politician who seeks to sell his politics by preaching religion, unless it be a preacher who tries to sell his sermons by talking politics." Yet he goes on to say that conservatism and religion cannot be kept in separate compartments, and that the true conservative at heart is a religious man. The social influence of Christianity has been nobly conservative, and a similarly conservative influence has been exerted by Buddhism, Islam, Judaism, and the other higher religions.

In America, a sense of religious consecration has been joined to our political institutions from the beginning. Almost all the signers of the Declaration of Independence and the delegates to the Constitutional Convention were religious men. Solemn presidential proclamations, since the beginning of the Republic, have invoked the might and mercy of God. Most of our leading conservative statesmen and writers were men profoundly religious—George Washington, an Episcopalian; John Adams, a Unitarian; James Madison, an Episcopalian; John Randolph, an Episcopalian; John C. Calhoun, a Unitarian; Orestes Brownson, a Catholic; Nathaniel Hawthorne, a Congregationalist; Abraham Lincoln, a devout though independent theist; and many more. "We know and we feel inwardly that religion is the basis of civil society, and the source of all good and all comfort," Edmund Burke wrote.

Now a conservative is a person who sees human society as an immortal contract between God and man, and between the generations that are dead, and the generation that is living now, and the generations which are yet to be born. It is possible to conceive of such a contract, and to feel a debt toward our ancestors and obligations toward our posterity, only if we are filled with a sense of eternal wisdom and power. We deal charitably and justly by our fellow men and women only because we believe that a divine will commands us to do so, and to love one another. The religious conservative is convinced that we have duties toward society, and that a just government is ruled by moral law, since we participate in our humble way in the divine nature and the divine love. The conservative believes that the fear of God is the beginning of wisdom.

The conservative desires to conserve human nature—that is, to keep men and women truly human, in God's image. The dread radical ideologies of our century, Communism and Nazism and their allies, endeavor to stamp out religion root and branch because they know that religion is always a barrier to collectivism and tyranny. A religious person has strength and faith; and radical collectivism detests private strength and faith. Throughout Europe and Asia, the real resistance to collectivism has come from men and women who believe that there is a greater authority than the collectivistic state, and that authority is God.

A society which denies religious truth lacks faith, charity, justice, and any sanction for its acts. Today, more perhaps than ever before, Americans understand the close connection between religious conviction and just government, so that they have amended their oath of allegiance to read, "one nation, *under God*." There is a divine power higher than any political power. When a nation ignores the divine authority, it soon commits the excesses of fanatic nationalism, intoxicated with its own unchecked power, which have made the twentieth century terrible.

Any religion is always in danger of corruption; and in our time, various people have endeavored to persuade us that the Christian religion endorses some sort of sentimental collectivism, a "religion of humanity," in which the Christian idea of equality in God's sight is converted into a dreary social and economic equality enforced by the state. But an examination of the Christian creeds and the Christian tradition will not sustain such an interpretation of Christian teaching. What Christianity offers is *personal* redemption, not some system of economic revolution. The human person is the great concern of Christian faith—as a person, not as part of a vague "People," or "The Masses," or "The Underprivileged." And when Christians preach charity, they mean the voluntary giving of those who have to those who have not; they do not mean compulsion by the state to take away from some in order to benefit others. "Statists that labor to contrive a commonwealth without poverty," old Sir Thomas Browne says, "take away the object of our charity; not understanding only the commonwealth of a Christian, but forgetting the prophecy of Christ." The Christian religion does indeed enjoin us to do unto others as we would have others do unto us; it does *not* enjoin us to employ political power to compel others to surrender their property.

Any great religion is assailed by heresies. In the year of the Communist Manifesto, Orestes Brownson declared that Communism is a heresy from Christianity; and he is echoed today by Arnold Toynbee and Eric Voegelin. Communism perverts the charity and love of Christianity into a fierce leveling doctrine that men must be made equal upon earth; at the same time, it denounces real equality, which is equality in the ultimate judgment of God. And other ideologies which would convert Christianity into an instrument for oppressing one class for the benefit of another are heresies.

Another distortion of Christianity is the radical doctrine that "the voice of the people is the voice of God." This, Lord Percy of Newcastle writes, is "the heresy of democracy"—that is, the disastrous error of supposing that God is simply whatever the majority of people think at any given time. The conservative knows that popular judgment commits blunder after blunder; it is anything but divine; while an immutable Justice which we perceive only imperfectly and dimly, and try to imitate in our human laws, is the real source of truth in politics.

A third perversion of Christianity is the heresy that this earthly society of ours can be made perfect, by world planners, and civil servants and enactments. The Christian knows that perfection, either in human beings or in society, never will be attained upon earth, but can be found only in a higher realm. This delusion of the possibility of earthly perfection lies behind most socialistic and totalitarian schemes. A professed Christian cannot be a professed Utopian. Our fallen nature, in the eyes of the sincere Christian, will not be redeemed until the end of all things; therefore, we are foolish if we expect that political and economic revolution will bring perfect justice and happiness. Men and women are creatures of mingled good and evil; in the best of us, some evil is present; and therefore, political constitutions, just laws, and social conventions are employed to restrain our evil impulses. Human beings without just and prudent government are delivered up to anarchy, for the brute lies just under the skin of civilization.

To presume to establish a synthetic paradise upon earth, predicated upon a fallaciously optimistic notion of human nature, will expose us to the peril of a reign of unreason. Vague schemes of world government ordinarily are afflicted by this folly. There never has been a perfect age or a perfect society, and there never will be, the religious conservative knows. All the political contrivances of mankind have been tried before, and none of them have worked to perfect satisfaction.

This is not to say that the religious conservative believes that all ages are the same, or that all evils are necessary evils. One age may be much worse than another; one society may be relatively just, and another relatively unjust; men may improve somewhat under a prudent and humane domination, and may deteriorate vastly in an insensate time. But the pseudo-gospel of Progress as the inevitable and beneficent wave of the future—a doctrine now shattered by the catastrophes of the twentieth century—never deluded the religious conservative. He does not despise the past simply because it is old, or assume that the present is delightful simply because it is ours. He judges every age and every institution in the light of certain principles of justice and order, which we have learnt in part through revelation and in part through the long and painful experience of the human race.

The religious thinker who criticizes our present society is not bound to maintain that one time is all white and another time is all black; he can pick and choose. If we pick and choose discreetly, we may hope to improve our own society considerably, though we never will succeed in making our society perfect. Human history is an account of men and women running as fast as they can, like Alice and the Red Queen, in order to stay where they are. Sometimes we grow lazy, and then society sinks into a terrible decline. We are never going to be able to run fast enough to arrive at Utopia. And we should hate Utopia if ever we got there, for it would be infinitely boring. What really makes men and women love life is the battle itself, the struggle to bring order out of disorder, to strive for right against evil. If ever that struggle should come to an end, we should expire of boredom. It is not in our nature to rest content, like the angels, in an eternal changelessness. In one sense, the religious conservative is a utopian, but in one sense only: he believes that the possibility of near-perfection does indeed exist, but it exists only within individual human persons; and when that state is attained individually, we call it sanctity.

Nor ought we to be discontented with this imperfect world of ours. G. K. Chesterton, in his "Ballad of the White Horse," tells of how King Alfred (a high-minded conservative some centuries before the word "conservative" was thought of) had a vision of the Virgin Mary; and when he asked her what of the future, Mary told him this:

> I tell you naught for your comfort,
>
> Yea, naught for your desire,
>
> Save that the sky grows darker yet
>
> And the sea rises higher.
>
> Night shall be thrice night over you,
>
> And heaven an iron cope.
>
> Do you have joy without a cause,
>
> Yea, faith without a hope?

Now these words made Alfred glad, for all their seeming grimness. For Alfred, as a Christian leader, knew that we are put here upon earth to struggle for the right, to contend against evil, and to defend the legacy of human nature and civilization. This is the conservative task in all ages; and, as Jefferson wrote, the tree of liberty must be watered from time to time with the blood of martyrs.

CHAPTER III

Conservatives and Conscience

I s a conservative a hardened egoist? Does he believe in unqualified "rugged individualism" to the exclusion of traditional duties toward God and man? In short, does the conservative have a conscience? The radical tells us that the conservative is a "wretch concentered all in self"; but I happen to have a different opinion.

"There is no necessary connection between knowledge and virtue," old John Adams wrote. "Simple intelligence has no association with morality. What connection is there between the mechanism of a clock or watch and the feeling of moral good and evil, right or wrong? A faculty or quality of distinguishing between normal good and evil, as well as physical happiness and misery, that is, pleasure and pain, or in other words a *conscience*—an old word almost out of fashion—is essential to morality."

If the good old word *conscience* was almost out of fashion when this Republic was founded, it has suffered still worse since then; and, as Adams knew, the whole world has suffered proportionately. Bentham endeavored to reduce "conscience" to mere enlightened selfishness; Marx declared that conscience had no function except as a weapon of the expropriated against the guilty expropriators; Freud thought that conscience was nothing better than guilt-complex derived principally from infantile mishaps. But as men and women denied any significance to the word and the concept of "conscience," the world began to experience the dismaying consequences of a philosophy that abandoned the ancient moral instrument of private responsibility, individual conscience, and tried to substitute instead some abstract "pleasure and pain" equation in morals, or some amorphous notion of "social justice" unrelated to personal duties and personal sense of abiding laws of right and wrong. The atrocities and catastrophes of our century, like those of Greece in the fifth century before Christ, demonstrate the pit into which fall sophisticated societies that mistake clever self-interest, or new "social controls," for a satisfactory alternative to conscience.

Now "conscience," in the dictionary's definition, is "the internal recognition of right and wrong as regards one's actions and motives; the faculty which decides upon the moral quality of one's actions and motives, enjoining one to conformity with the moral law." Conscience is a private matter: there is really no such thing as a "public conscience" or a "state conscience." Conscience has two aspects: one governing the relationship between God and the individual human person, and the other governing the relationship between one human person and his fellow men and women. The great majority of conservatives—men and women who were not born yesterday, and are not afraid of acknowledging that our ancestors were something better than fools—believe in the reality of conscience, quite as they believe in the reality of religious truth.

All during the twentieth century, radicals have been trying to convince the thinking public that conservatives are enemies of conscience. The conservative is a monster of selfishness, according to the radical propagandist: the conservative believes in "devil take the hindmost," the radical insists; he believes in greed on principle, his heart is hardened against the weak and unfortunate in the race of life, and when he talks of duties and rights, this is a mere veneer over selfish interests. Conservatives, the radical proclaims, are somehow morally impure, ruthless, and avaricious, dedicated to the proposition that "they shall take who have the power, and they shall keep who can."

Yet the real position of the thinking conservative is quite the opposite of this radical caricature. Of course, there are selfish and heartless conservatives, just as there are selfish and heartless radicals: political persuasion cannot of itself produce private virtue, and we are all of us in some degree sinners, whatever ticket we vote. This said, however, the theory of the thinking conservative, and ordinarily his practice, run all in favor of private conscience, with the rights and duties toward God and toward mankind which a serious conscience requires in any society and any age. It is the doctrinaire radical of modern times, rather, who denies the divine source of conscience and the sense of personal responsibility and traditional duty which gives conscience meaning. Some people calling themselves conservatives are afflicted with the vice of selfishness, arrogant pride of possession—just as some people calling themselves radicals are afflicted with the vice of envy, lusting after their neighbors' goods. But we are talking here of social principles, not of individual failings.

It has been said by a hostile critic that the conservative believes all social questions to be at bottom questions of private morality. Properly understood, this is quite true; and thinking conservatives can take a modest pride in this conviction. A society in which men and women are governed by conscience, by a strong sense of moral right and wrong, by private convictions of honor and justice, will be a good society, the conservative thinks, whatever political machinery it may utilize; while a society in which men and women are morally adrift, ignorant of conscience, and intent only upon gratification of sensual desires, will be a bad society, no matter how many people vote and no matter how "liberal" its formal constitution may be. For justice and generosity in any nation are no better and no worse than the prevailing private convictions of the men and women who compose that nation. Soviet Russia may have a model constitution, in the eyes of the doctrinaire radical; but justice and generosity are nearly dead in Soviet Russia, because conscience is left out of question. Britain may have a very antiquated constitution, in the eyes of the doctrinaire radical; but justice and generosity are very much alive in Britain, because the influence of private conscience remains pervasive.

As the modern radical has come to disregard private responsibility in morals and politics and economic life, so he has come to depreciate the idea of private conscience. All the same, he knows there is power left in the word "conscience," and he cannot be wholly unaware that a society decays if it recognizes no enduring standards of right and wrong: so, endeavoring to warp the word to fit his ideology, the radical frequently talks of "social conscience." But he rarely defines this phrase; one gathers its meaning only by the context in which the radical puts it. By "social conscience," the radical seems to imply a belief that one person ought somehow to feel guilty about being in any way superior to anyone else—and, more, that somehow an abstract justice dictates to mankind the right and duty to pull everyone down to a dead level of equality. I am aware that I am not being fair to all radicals when I write this: some radicals do mean something better when they say "social conscience"—they mean the traditional obligation of those favored in this world to assist those who have been unfortunate. But I cannot perceive how this latter usage of "social conscience" has any advantage over that simple old word "conscience." Conscience always has dictated charity. And I am afraid that *most* radicals want simply to pull down political establishments and private property and superior private abilities when they talk of "social conscience."

The conservative never has erected a wall between private conscience and society. Aside from the obligations toward God and one's self which conscience dictates, the whole function of conscience is to teach us how to deal justly with our fellow men and women. And society is simply our fellow men and women considered collectively. There cannot be one kind of conscience for dealing with the men and women we meet, as persons—and a second kind of conscience for dealing with abstract "society," as if somehow society were not made up of individual human beings. Conscience is simply conscience. It is not "social" or "anti-social." It is the sense of right and justice which instructs us how we, as moral persons, ought to live with other moral persons.

So, the conservative is not "anti-social" or "conscience-less." The thinking conservative believes that conscience is healthy in proportion as it touches directly upon particular human beings whom we know, and unhealthy in proportion as it becomes abstract, sentimental, generalized, institutionalized, and directed by impersonal political authority. Many of the people who "bestow a kiss upon the universe" and talk windily of "social conscience" are the least reliable guardians of right and wrong when they come face to face with private duties and their neighbors. Conservatism has been called "loyalty to persons," as against abstract ideological attachment to impersonal establishments and theoretic dogma. Just so, the conservative is conscientious because he respects the truly human person, the moral individual. He is charitable precisely because he knows that charity begins at home; he is just precisely because he looks upon men and women as his brothers and sisters, under a divine commandment of love, not as units in an efficient planned economy.

Good old-fashioned conscience always has impelled men and women to be charitable. ("Charity," literally understood, means "tenderness," not simply "relief.") It has always taught the strong, the wise, the industrious, the provident, the fortunate, the swift, the handsome, the inheritor of wealth, to assist from the charity of their hearts, and to the full extent of their ability, our fellow men and women who are weak or unfortunate or sick or old or bewildered. In this sense, conscience always has been "social." The conservative does not need any new dispensation to inform him of his charitable duties. But he is convinced that the way to a good conscience is through *personal* charity, *personal* relationships, and *private* duties—not, ordinarily, through the mechanical and impersonal functioning of some grandiose state design. He wants to keep conscience, like charity, close to home; because once conscience ceases to be personal, it ceases to be conscience at all, being transformed into nothing better than enlightened selfishness or positive law. He recognizes that, in some matters and in cases of emergency, private conscience must work collectively, through public agencies. But, understanding the nature of conscience, he tries to keep, to the fullest extent possible, the operation of conscience as a personal and private matter.

When the conservative engages in charity, for instance, he first endeavors to do all that he can personally and privately. When that will not suffice—when self-help and family cooperation are not enough—he turns to private voluntary agencies. When these, in their turn, do not seem sufficient, he resorts to municipal and local and state action. If all these resources somehow fail, then he turns to charity on a national scale. But he is inclined to believe that all the ordinary problems of society, except in great emergencies, can be dealt with sufficiently, and most humanely, on the personal, local, voluntary foundation of simple conscience, the sense of duty which good men and women feel toward their fellow-creatures. If that healthy private conscience sinks into apathy or vice, there is no use talking about "social conscience": there cannot be a nation in which private morality is bad and public morality is good.

Chapter IV

Conservatives and Individuality

"Individualism," like "capitalism," is a word coined by the socialists. By it, the nineteenth-century socialists meant to imply that while the socialist is concerned with "society"—that is, the welfare of everyone—the conservative is an "individualist," selfishly concerned only with himself. This caricature of the conservative has done much mischief. I think it is important to understand what the real conservative believes about human individuality and private rights.

The word "individualism" is very loosely used nowadays in the United States, and some people of conservative opinions do themselves and their cause harm by speaking and writing as if the conservative indeed were selfish on principle, as the socialist says the "individualist" is. As a term of political science, "individualist"—that is, a person who subscribes unreservedly to "individualism," the political ideology—means a disciple of William Godwin, Thomas Hodgskin, and Herbert Spencer. Now Godwin and Hodgskin were doctrinaire radicals, and Spencer—though there are conservative elements in some of his writings—never would have thought of calling himself a conservative.

An Individualist of the school of Godwin and Hodgskin believes that every man is a law unto himself, that established social institutions—particularly the established forms of private property—are irrational, that traditional religion and traditional morality are mostly nonsense, and that every man should do in every respect just as he pleases. Now whatever may be said of these notions, they certainly are not conservative; and so Americans of conservative inclinations who call themselves "Individualists" run the risk of confusing the whole discussion and bringing conservatism into disrepute. They may play directly into the hands of the socialists, who declare that the conservative is a heartless individualist, and therefore devoted to ruthless competition, perfectly selfish, and hostile toward everything charitable and venerable in the world. A real conservative, however, cannot be a real individualist. The thoroughgoing individualist, in the strict sense of that term, is hostile toward religion, toward patriotism, toward the inheritance of property, and toward the past. A conservative, on the contrary, is a friend to religious belief, to national loyalty, to established rights in society, and to the wisdom of our ancestors.

I have been speaking above of the strict meaning of the political term "individualism." The conservative, however, is an individualist in the sense that he believes in the primacy of the individual, the right of the human person to be himself. When there is a conflict between overweening claims of the political state and the rights of individuals, the conservative is on the side of the individual. He is opposed to the theory of Hegel that the State somehow exists independently of the individual human persons who make up society. The conservative believes that government is a contrivance of human wisdom, under Providence, to provide for human wants. The chief of those human wants are justice, order, and freedom. If a political state begins to neglect the rights of individual persons, and sets up some system of "dictatorship of the proletariat" or "democratic despotism" or "mass state," then the conservative sets his face against this usurpation of authority. For the conservative thinks that a just government guarantees to individuals all the liberty that is consonant with justice and order. The function of the just state is to increase personal freedom under law, not to decrease it. If, in the name of an abstract "general welfare," the state reduces the ordered liberty of every citizen, then the conservative takes up the cause of individuality, with resolution.

I think, in short, that the conservative is all in favor of individuality, private rights, variety in society; and that the conservative is equally opposed to "Individualism" as a radical political ideology, and to political systems that would make the individual merely a servant of the state. The wise government, in the conservative's view, tries to insure two great principles relative to human personality. The first of these principles is that the men and women of remarkable minds and abilities ought to be protected in their right to develop and unfold their unusual personalities. The second of these principles is that the men and women in the ordinary walks of life, who do not have the ability or the wish to accomplish remarkable things, ought to be protected in their right to proceed in the placid round of their duties and enjoyments, unoppressed by the people of remarkable abilities. These two principles, the conservative thinks, are calculated to shelter and nourish true and healthy individuality. The conservative believes that men and women, though equal before the law, are very different in their capacities and their desires. Some men and some women are filled with ambition, energy, and remarkable qualities of mind and heart; these people ought to be allowed to develop their talents to the full, provided that they do not infringe upon the rights of other people. But other men and women—and these are the majority of mankind—prefer to live quietly, regularly, and securely; and these men and women ought to be allowed to live as they like, provided they do not try to force the energetic or talented people to submit to their tastes and their pleasures. When the rights of both these groups are secured, then a society has a just government, and human individuality is properly recognized.

So, the real conservative is neither a selfish "individualist" (in the invidious phrase of the socialist), trampling on the rights and wishes of his neighbors; nor is he a dull collectivist, intent upon reducing all men and women to some dead-level of mind and condition. The conservative wants people to be different; for a world in which everyone was the same would be infinitely boring, and would sink down to its own destruction. There are some things, however, in which people ought to be substantially the same. They ought to subscribe to the same general moral principles, and they ought to pay a common respect to the legacy of their civilization, and they ought to feel a common loyalty to the social institutions which give them justice and order and freedom. The conservative is not afraid of being called a "conformist" in these great matters. And when the radical revolutionary or the rootless bohemian endeavors to subvert these moral and social conventions, then the conservative does not hesitate to condemn an "individuality" which would end in the destruction of civilized life.

I mean that the conservative is not an anarchist. He believes that just government—like the constitutional government of the United States, with its checks and balances and its guarantees of private rights—is a great force for good. The signers of the Declaration of Independence and the members of the Constitutional Convention were not individualists—emphatically not—in the sense of believing that men and women are made free or happy simply by destroying all old moral and political institutions. On the contrary, the Founding Fathers designed to establish "a more perfect union" in which individual personality would thrive precisely because good constitutions and prudent government would restrain the anarchic impulse in human nature. Simply doing as one likes, without respect for the rights and wishes of one's neighbors, is not true freedom; and it does not lead to real development of the higher human personality, but leads instead to a primitive state of life, "poor, nasty, brutish, and short."

And I mean, further, that the conservative is not a collectivist. He believes that men and women are free in proportion as they are able, and are expected, to make their own choices in life. He does not want an insect-society in which the wills of the great mass of people are made subject to the decisions of an oligarchy. He thinks that the state exists to provide for the justice and order and freedom of individual human persons—not that individuals exist simply to serve an abstract state. He thinks that men and women never are truly human if their decisions are made for them by an omnipotent political authority. He desires to see the rich, invigorating, interesting variety of a society in which every man or woman—subject only to the moral law and to the moderate restraints of a limited government—is able to be "his own potty little self."

The conservative knows that freedom without any restraints may lead to oppression or anarchy, just as government without any restraints may lead to collectivism. But he believes the best and most effective restraint upon anarchic individualism to be obedience to moral law, the private conscience, rather than a regular and vexatious exercise of the police-power of political authority. He does not think that government, of itself, can successfully regulate selfishness, egoism, and the lust for power in human hearts. We might pass a most complicated bill giving the state authority to interfere in every walk of private life so as to eliminate selfishness, vainglory, and power-hunger; and yet such a code probably would simply aggravate the evils it was intended to repress. For a society is good only in proportion as the individuals within it are good and truly free, under the moral law.

Individuality without moral restraints or just laws often has led to selfish excess; there are many such instances in the history of our country. Yet the conservative prefers to try to bring about the reform of "ruthless individualism" by operating upon the private conscience rather than by calling into operation a police state. The only way to check selfishness, Aristotle says, is "to train the nobler sort of natures not to desire more." And the only real way to check envy is to remind the mass of men and women that unusual talents have their rights, as well as ordinary talents. Irving Babbitt, a generation ago, expressed the conservative's view in this matter with a high dignity:

The remedy for such a failure of the man at the top to curb his desires does not lie, as the agitator would have us believe, in inflaming the desires of the man at the bottom; nor again in substituting for real justice some phantasmagoria of social justice. As a result of such a substitution, one will presently be turning from the punishment of the individual offender to an attack on the institution of property itself; and a war on capital will speedily degenerate, as it always has in the past, into a war on thrift and industry in favor of laziness and incompetence, and finally into schemes of confiscation that profess to be idealistic and are in fact subversion of common honesty. Above all, social justice is likely to be unsound in its partial or total suppression of competition. Without competition it is impossible that the ends of true justice should be fulfilled—namely, that every man should receive according to his works. The principle of competition, as Hesiod pointed out long ago, is built into the very roots of the world; there is something in the nature of things that calls for a real victory and a real defeat. Competition is necessary to rouse man from his native indolence; without it, life loses its zest and savor. Only, as Hesiod goes on to say, there are two types of competition—the one that leads to bloody war and the other that is the mother of enterprise and high achievement.

Thus the conservative is dedicated to true individuality, the right and the duty of men and women to be themselves; the conservative seeks enlightened competition, differences of rank and station and wealth, life with variety and even with risk. But he does not seek a doctrinaire "Individualism" that favors selfishness, private illicit ambition, and "devil take the hintermost" on principle. He does not seek this any more than he seeks a stifling collectivism. He thinks that society ought to foster true individuality, and that the proper checks upon a ruthless individualism are private conscience and good constitutions, not constant and direct political surveillance of our economy and our private lives. The conservative is not an ideologue; that is, he does not yearn for complete moral and political anarchy, or for a total "welfare state" opposed to individual variety. He thinks that our old established American society, in which private ambition and public order are reconciled and mutually checked, offers us the general solution to the problem of the individual versus the state.

No society ever puts an end, once and for all, to the conflicting claims of ordered government and private ambition. The best we can hope for is a society in which men and women recognize the general principle that the superior natures are entitled to develop themselves, and that the average natures are entitled to live in tranquility. There was a time, in the history of our country, when it seemed that ruthless individualism might overthrow this principle. But that time is gone by; and at present, the danger is rather that the state may repress true individuality in the name of a leveling "social justice." Nowadays, therefore, the prudent conservative endeavors to redress the balance by supporting, with all the strength at his command, the rights of the individual against the arrogant demands of the mass state.

CHAPTER V

Conservatives and the Family

"The germ of public affections," Burke wrote, "is to learn to love the little platoon we belong to in society." We cannot feel any affection for our country unless we first love those near to us. The conservative feels that the family is the natural source and core of any good society; that when the family decays, a dreary collectivism is sure to supplant it; and that the principal instrument of moral instruction, ordinary education, and satisfactory economic life always must remain the family. What makes life worth living is love; and love is learnt in the family, and withers when the health of family-life is impaired.

Now very powerful forces are at work to diminish the influence of the family among us, and even to destroy the family for all purposes except mere generation. Some of these forces are material and unintentional: certain aspects of modern industrialism, which break up the old economic unity of the family; cheap amusements and transportation, which encourage members of the family to spend nearly all their time outside the family circle; the assumption of the old educational functions of the family by public schools, in considerable part. The real conservative seeks to modify or reverse these tendencies by reminding men and women that family love is more important than material gain; and he tries to devise practical means to reconcile family unity with the demands of modern life.

But other forces hostile to the family are not merely impersonal and unconscious: they are more or less deliberate, and they may be countered by intelligent action in the social and educational and political spheres. The chief of these ominous forces is the deliberate desire of certain people to have the political state assume nearly all the responsibilities which the family once possessed. This movement is the most thorough and disastrous form of collectivism. That some of the people who advocate such a course are well-intentioned does not excuse their design. We all know what hell is paved with. A distinguished historical sociologist, Dr. R. A. Nisbet, in his *Quest for Community*, describes the scheme of the totalitarians, the Nazis and the Communists, for extirpating the family:

> The shrewd totalitarian mentality knows well the powers of intimate kinship and religious devotion for keeping alive in a population values and incentives which might well, in the future, serve as the basis of resistance. Thus to emancipate each member, and especially the younger members, from the family was an absolute necessity. And this planned spiritual alienation from kinship was accomplished, not only through the

negative processes of spying and informing, but
through the sapping of the functional foundations of family membership and through the substitution of new and attractive political roles for
each of the social roles embodied in the family
structure. The techniques varied. But what was
essential was the atomization of the family and
of every other type of grouping that intervened
between the people as society and the people as
a mindless, soulless, traditionless mass. What the
totalitarian must have for the realization of his
design is a spiritual and cultural vacuum.

George Orwell, in his novel *1984,* describes London children taught to spy systematically on their parents, and
approved for bringing about their destruction. This final disintegration of family love, and all love, already is a reality in
the nations dominated by the Communists. And if the family
continues to decay in the rest of the world, such a culmination
is conceivable even in our society.

Some of the deliberate or quasi-deliberate techniques of
the mass-state for undermining the family are these:

1. Taking the instruction of children entirely
   away from their parents by the official adoption of theories that prescribe "educating the
   whole child" in the state schools, with a cor-
   responding depreciation of parental intelligence and rights.

2. Creating "youth organizations" to take young people quite out of the sphere of the family in their leisure hours, and to indoctrinate them in the ideology of the mass-state.

3. Abolishing the inheritance of family property, through confiscatory inheritance taxes or through income tax policies that leave small margin for family saving.

4. Planned encouragement of divorce, "sexual freedom," and "deprivatization of women," through positive legislation or official propaganda, with the aim of weakening the bonds of affection within the family that offer a strong barrier to the wishes of the total state.

And there are yet other ways in which political authority is employed to make the family into a mere household—and into only a fragile and impersonal household, at that. Against these deliberate attacks on the family, as against the less deliberate assaults of modern life, the conservative sets his face. He knows that if the family is to survive, thinking men and women who believe the family to be a great power for good must take prompt countermeasures. He knows, with Professor Pitirim Sorokin, that the family must be restored and reconstructed among us, not merely praised in vague terms. As Dr. Sorokin writes:

The family ... should become again a union of bodies, souls, hearts, and minds in a single collective 'we.' Its basic function, that of inculcating deep sympathy, compassion, love, and loyalty in its members, not only in relation to one another but toward humanity at large, must be restored and fully developed. This is necessary because no other agency can perform this function as well as the average good family. This type of family will become the cornerstone of a new creative social order.

For, as Dr. Sorokin suggests, the intelligent conservative does not simply stand still. In this age particularly, tradition and established institutions are being broken up by terrible forces, and the conservative has to look into the future, as well as study the past, if he is to conserve the best in our heritage. He must restore the family in order to keep the family from extinction. He may create a new and better social order, not by cooperating in the grim process of social collectivization, but by infusing new life into the ancient and well-loved institutions of family, church, and community. The family is true voluntary community, inspired by love and common understanding. The only alternative to the family is the total state, governed by force and central power.

The conservative is in favor of many kinds of freedom. He supports, for example, political liberty, under just and balanced constitutions; economic liberty, under the rules of morality; intellectual liberty, balanced by a sense of intellectual responsibility. But there are alleged "freedoms" that the thinking conservative knows to be anarchical and malevolent. He does not recognize any natural freedom to take someone else's goods, or to subvert law and order, or to demolish the moral principles which have created true freedom itself. And he denies that any person, or any collective body, rightfully enjoys the freedom to break down all the subtle ties of affection and interest that have created the family. Such an appetite is not liberty, but license. Demands for reducing marriage to a mere legal form of sexual union, if even that; for converting man and woman into a mere blur, with identical functions and tasks; for "liberating" the child from the influence of his parents; for abandoning the moral precepts which are the accumulated wisdom of the race, in favor of some collectivistic "new morality"—these demands are not part of ordered liberty, but are the negation of true freedom.

The family is more than a simple arrangement for the gratification of sexual impulses, and more than a mere housing-device. As Dr. Sorokin says, "More successfully than any other group, it has transformed its members into a single entity, with a common fund of values, with common joys and sorrows, spontaneous cooperation and willing sacrifice." It keeps sterile collectivism at bay. It teaches us the meaning of love and duty, and what it is to be a true man or a true woman. It is the primary "little platoon we belong to in society." The conservative knows that, the family lacking, nothing very important in our culture can be preserved or improved. The traditional family—which, like many old-fashioned things, is an indispensable thing—gives us those roots without which we all would be just so many lonely little atoms of humanity, unprincipled and at the mercy of some iron political domination.

CHAPTER VI

Conservatives and the Community

A solitary man, Aristotle says, must be either a beast or a god. Since not many of us are godlike, we live in communities, lest we grow bestial. Community is a great good; it makes civilization and moral growth possible; and when community weakens, it is replaced not by anarchic freedom, ordinarily, but by a stifling collectivism. Aristotle reminds us that we are naturally gregarious, taking pleasure in other people's company. Therefore, the man who disrupts the true community is depriving us of a great part of our human nature.

Although we Americans have always been intensely attached to privacy and private rights, we also have been a nation conspicuous for a hearty and successful spirit of community. Our city, township, and county governments; our flourishing voluntary associations; our innumerable fraternal and charitable bodies—these are the forms which have been realized by our desire for true community. Tocqueville found the genuine desire to serve and promote the community stronger among us than in Europe, despite our American proclivity for moving about. It is this combination of local independence with neighborliness and voluntary association that has made possible what Orestes Brownson called "territorial democracy" in the United States—that is, local free government, as distinguished from the centralized and fanatical democracies that arose in Europe out of the French Revolution.

Now real community is detested by the radical social reformer, in our century, who would like to see society forced into a single rigid mold, characterized by central administration, rule through executive decree, uniformity of life, and eradication of all personal and local distinctions. The radical—especially the Marxist—knows that healthy community is the enemy of his schemes, for community encourages variety of opinion and custom, sheltering all those voluntary associations which oppose centralized despotism. Accordingly, the radical doctrinaire, once he is in power, endeavors to stamp out the vigor of local community, as Hitler tried to do in Germany, and as the Communists have done with dismaying thoroughness in Russia and elsewhere.

The radical reformer is not the only enemy of true community nowadays. Certain great blind tendencies in modern technology and economic life also threaten traditional community—the centralization of production and distribution, the decay of rural patterns of living, the excessive mobility of population, the standardization of amusements and customs, the well-meant (though mistaken) drift in many quarters toward consolidation of local political and charitable functions into state and federal bureaucracies. Against these influences, more subtle though less directly malign than revolutionary political doctrines, the intelligent conservative contends.

The true conservative is public-spirited: he believes in community. That does not mean that he is in any sense a collectivist. The public-spirited man or woman, in this country, believes in a Republic, a nation in which nearly all activities are carried on voluntarily, by private individuals or local groups, for the general benefit. The collectivist, on the contrary, believes in a Mass-State, a consolidated unitary domination in which compulsion is the order of the day, and in which every aspect of life is regulated by some central body, theoretically for the general benefit, but really for the benefit of some clique or class. If community is disrupted, then collectivism usurps the functions which community formerly exercised, and return to voluntary community becomes next to impossible.

In a genuine community, the decisions which most directly affect the lives of citizens are made locally and voluntarily: the administration of justice, the police function, the maintenance of roads and public buildings and communal amenities, the assessment and collection of taxes, the management of charities and hospitals, the establishment of schools, the supervision of economic development. Some of these functions are carried out by local political bodies, and others by private associations: so long as they are kept local, and are marked by the general agreement of the citizens, they constitute healthy community. But when they pass by default or usurpation to centralized authority, then community is in grave danger—and, with community, private rights and social well-being are in peril. Whatever is beneficent and prudent in modern democracy is made possible through vital community-sense. If, in the name of an abstract "Democracy," the functions of community are assigned to central authority, then real government by the consent of the governed gives way to an impersonal leveling and standardizing process that is hostile to freedom and human dignity.

The influences which make community healthy still are strong in America. We have more voluntary organizations than has any other nation; we generally are jealous of our local rights; we retain a constitutional structure which puts formidable impediments in the way of the radical reformer who would crush society into an amorphous mass. Yet we cannot afford to be complacent. Community can be lost in a fit of public absence of mind.

For it is tempting and easy to let centralized power assume the burdens which necessarily accompany the privileges of community. To escape the demands of local taxation, we may tolerate an increasing shift of the costs of schooling, public improvements, charitable functions, and even police-functions to state and national administration. In some respects, we are already far gone on this road. In the earlier stages of this process, it may seem that we have retained most of the benefits of community even though we have shifted to other shoulders the responsibilities that the community has long performed. It may take decades or generations for the consequences of this surrender of rights and duties to make itself fully felt. Yet the consequences of the process, if that process is not arrested, may be predicted by anyone with some knowledge of history. The late Albert Jay Nock, in his *Memoirs of a Superfluous Man,* suggested the usual course of events:

> Closer centralization; a steadily growing bureaucracy;
> State power and faith in State power increasing, social
> power and faith in social power diminishing; the State

absorbing a continually larger proportion of the national
income; production languishing; the State in consequence taking over one 'essential industry' after another,
managing them with ever-increasing corruption, inef-
ficiency, and prodigality, and finally resorting to a system of forced labor. Then at some point in this process
a collision of State interests, at least as general and as
violent as that which occurred in 1914, will result in an
industrial and financial dislocation too severe for the
asthenic social structure to bear; and from this the State
will be left to 'the rusty death of machinery' and the
casual anonymous forces of dissolution.

I may add that this disintegration of community, and its sup-
planting by centralized authority, commonly have been accompanied by a proportionate decay of culture and morality, which
seem to flourish only when local community teaches men and
women standards of civilization and decency.

For a nation is no stronger than the numerous little communities of which it is composed. A central administration, or a corps
of select managers and civil servants, however well-intentioned and
well-trained, cannot confer justice and prosperity and tranquility
and decent conduct upon a mass of men and women deprived of
their traditional responsibilities and institutions. That experiment
has been made before, notably in ancient Rome; and it has been
disastrous. It is the performance of our duties which teaches us
responsibility and prudence and efficiency and charity and morality. If someone else assumes these duties, or is forced to shoulder
them, then we atrophy, socially and morally, for lack of exercise.

And the bureaucracy which has assumed those social responsibilities, besides, does not long remain high-minded and diligent; the managers and civil servants must be recruited from the society in which they live; they cannot escape corruption and indolence, if they have their being in a time of disintegrated community.

Doubtless it often is vexatious to serve on local school boards, or to have to attend the meetings of private charitable societies, or to pay for local improvements out of local funds, or to put down crime through local reform. But if these duties are shifted from the community to some centralized agency, before long true community will cease to exist. And, some form of cooperative action being necessary to every civilized people, we shall not go back to the days of the Noble Savage: we shall find ourselves thrust, rather, into an epoch of collectivism. That new domination may seem beneficent at first; but it will be neither efficient nor mild, after the elapse of some years.

So, the thinking conservative does his duty by his community—his town, his country, his business-organization, his civic association, his union, his church-group, his professional body, his school or university, and his charitable fund. All these are parts of real community. He does not believe that he will have done his duty as a citizen if he merely votes for positive legislation calculated to let someone else, afar off, perform all the functions of these vital associations. Community is essential to freedom, to private rights, and to the whole fabric of the civil social order. Without it, men and women become less than human—either the solitary beasts of Aristotle's phrase, or the servile mass-people of the unitary state. The conservative does not pose as an anarchist, despising his duties toward other men. And he does not propose to exchange his birthright of community for the pottage of centralized Utopia.

CHAPTER VII

Conservatives and Just Government

J efferson called government a necessary evil; but most
Americans never really believed that; and, in the eyes of
conservatives generally, government is a necessary
good—so long as it is just, constitutional, balanced, restricted
government. Justice, order, and freedom are dependent upon
a satisfactory balance between governmental authority and
private rights. In times of anarchy, the thinking conservative
endeavors to support the claims of just government; in times
of frowning centralization and consolidation of political
power, the thinking conservative turns to the defense of the
individual against the state. In our age and our country, the
latter tendency is at work, so that the American conservative
nowadays seeks to restrain the influence of governmental
agencies, rather than to buttress the political authority.

In the years which intervened between the achievement of
American independence and the adoption of the Federal Constitution, matters were otherwise. Then the danger was that the
loose American Confederation would break asunder, and that
authority might fall into the hands of adventurers, radical fac-
tions, or foreign powers. Our Federal Constitution, which Sir

Henry Maine called the great political achievement of modern times, was framed to put an end to this peril; and that Constitution, comparatively little altered, has helped immeasurably ever since to conserve our ordered liberty.

Just government rarely is the hasty creation of a few ingenious men: instead, it is the consequence of a slow growth, the experience of a nation under Providence. Now and then a vigorous reformer may accelerate this progress or some mistaken reformer may injure a nation's constitution; but, by and large, the sound institutions of any nation are the product of historical experience. This is true of the United States of America, even though our Constitution seems, at first glance, to have been got up in the space of a few months at Philadelphia. For our federal constitution, like our original state constitutions, was founded upon a century and a half of practical colonial experience of the governance of men; and back of that lay six hundred years and more of English experience; while the whole legacy of classical and Christian civilization contributed to our ideas of just constitutions. The Jewish understanding of morality; the Roman idea of law; the Christian concept of the dignity of man: all these were in the minds of the framers of our Constitution. Strong, pious, and practical men, many of them learned, the founders of the Republic did not presume to create out of whole cloth the real constitution of our country. They merely expressed formally the historical experience and the moral precepts of the civilization and the land to which they belonged. They were justly proud of creating a new nation; but they also were humble before the wisdom of our ancestors. In *The Federalist Papers,* perhaps the finest expression of practical statecraft of modern times, Madison, Hamilton, and Jay drew upon the storehouse of history and of English and colonial experience for their proofs. In his *Defense of the Constitutions,* John Adams reviewed the course of politics from the early Greek states down to the eighteenth century, explaining that American government was a prudent development, justified by the lessons of many centuries; and when the French reformer Condorcet praised Americans for having created something entirely new, on abstract principles, Adams wrote, "Fool! Fool!" For John Adams, like most of the other founders of the Republic, knew that the only really just government is that which grows out of the moral and social experience of the race.

In our age, the most successful examples of just government have been the English and the American. British government now appears to be undergoing profound, if subtle, transformations, the consequence of the drifting of all authority into the hands of Parliament or the civil service. American government, however, despite the increase of federal activities, remains recognizably what its founders intended it to be: the essence of our constitution has survived the party battles of six generations. Generally we have abstained from presumptuous tinkering with a form of government that has worked well: we have not been ideologues, or coffee-house philosophers, afflicted with the delusion that our petty private rationality is superior to the experience of the nation. Attachment to our federal principle—to the constitution which reconciles state and local rights with union for the common security—has dominated the thought of most of our principal statesmen: Calhoun or Webster, Lincoln or Douglas. The interpretation of the

Constitution, or of what prudent policy ought to be, has varied widely; but affection for the general concepts which underlie our government has remained constant.

Nowadays, however, certain social and economic and military changes in our life, and the arguments of a school of thinkers who prefer consolidation to local and private liberties, challenge the whole basis of our constitutional structure. We are told by some that our historical experience is obsolete. Professor Hartz, of Harvard, insists that "instead of recapturing our past, we have got to transcend it. As for a child who is leaving adolescence, there is no going home again for America." And Professor Hofstadter, of Columbia, tells us that "in a corporate and consolidated society demanding international responsibility, cohesion, centralization, and planning, the traditional ground is shifting under our feet." They, and others, imply that the whole set of moral principles, philosophical postulates, and constitutional establishments upon which our society rests must be replaced by some new domination. The conservative thinker, however, denies these assertions; with Professor Rossiter, of Cornell, he says, "Americans may eventually take the advice of their advanced philosophers and adopt a political theory that pays more attention to groups, classes, public opinion, power-elites, positive law, public administration, and other realities of twentieth-century America. Yet it seems safe to predict that the people, who occasionally prove themselves wiser than their philosophers, will go on thinking about the political community in terms of inalienable rights, popular sovereignty, consent, constitutionalism, separation of powers, morality, and limited government. The political theory of the American Revolution—a theory of ethical, ordered liberty—remains the political tradition of the American people."

Those who incline toward the latter point of view need to understand clearly just what the chief principles of prescriptive government in America are. I think that two cardinal ideas have taken form in our political structure, from colonial times to the present:

1. The belief that men and women have a natural right to make their own decisions in most walks of life; therefore the powers of government are sharply defined and delimited. Just government is intended to secure to all men and women the private rights which make possible a high civil social order. When government encroaches upon those private rights, that government ceases to be just. There always will be a debate over exactly where private rights end and public interests begin; but the general American assumption has been that the citizen surrenders in trust to the state—that is, to local, state, or federal authority—only such powers as are necessary for the common welfare. The American theory has been that moral and political authority resides in individual human persons, under God, and not in an abstract state. Therefore, the people have conferred upon the state only such powers as are necessary for the common defense and convenience,

and have watched jealously over the exercise of those powers.

2. The belief that our Republic ought to be what Orestes Brownson called it, a "territorial democracy"—that is, a nation characterized by the reservation of governmental power chiefly to local and state authorities; power is only delegated to the federal government. This is limited, "filtered" democracy, a world away from the leveling and unrestricted democracy of Rousseau and the French Revolutionaries. We have been democrats only in the sense that we have believed that the common concerns of the people ought to be considered, in most instances, locally; that public decisions ought to be made by the free will of free citizens, meeting together on a human scale. We never have embraced the theory that a centralized democracy, a democracy without constitutional limitation, can be a just and free government. Our government has worked well because its policies have been concerted by little groups of private citizens, making their choices locally and then influencing national action through their constituted representatives. Our government has been a just and free government because of its elaborate system of checks and balances, which generally has prevented intolerant majorities or selfish minorities from imposing their will upon

the nation at large. We have deliberately abstained from concentrating power in the national capital or in the executive—though the slow drift of events now has established in Washington, nevertheless, such heavy responsibilities that neither President nor Congress can deal adequately with them. We never have indulged the illusion that any man or any little body of men, acting from some political center, can beneficently administer the concerns of local communities and private individuals.

Concern for natural private rights; concern for representative and *federal*—not central—government: these have been the political principles upon which the United States have remained a model to friends of justice, order, and freedom throughout the world. I think it dangerous to tamper with the foundations of this elaborate edifice. Nations are like trees: it will not do to hack at their roots, though we may prune their branches.

I doubt whether the people who exhort us to transcend our political traditions really understand the consequences of altering radically the assumptions and institutions upon which a successful government has been founded. In "transcending" our intricate traditions and constitutions that are derived from Christian faith and from the civil social experience of English and American history, they would soon find themselves confronted by the necessity of recognizing or establishing some alternative set of traditions and constitutions. These radical reformers do not present any such set of traditions and constitutions. Most of them have now disavowed Marxism; they are aware in some degree of the deficiencies of old-fashioned rationalism and positivism; they are a little embarrassed about socialism; they are even beginning to confess the insufficiency of doctrinaire liberalism. Yet they exhibit prejudices against our prescriptive territorial democracy; they talk of planning, centralization, unification; they imply that they would like to create some sort of elite of centralizers and planners, presumably governed by the vague aspirations of "democratic socialism."

But men do not live and die by the speculations of "democratic socialism." The man who respects the historical experience of his country prefers the devil he knows to the devil he doesn't. He is not disposed to sweep away a body of institutions and beliefs that has served us well in exchange for some new domination of opinions and laws to which its authors cannot even give a name. The American political system has preserved to the American people a very high degree of justice and order and freedom—higher, perhaps, than that of any other nation, with the possible exception of Britain. We may judge a government by its fruits. Our political system has been remarkably fruitful; and the prudent social reformer, I think, will make his amendments in consonance with that political tradition, for the sake of giving old constitutions renewed vitality. His only alternative is to sweep all the pieces off the board. But then he will not be playing the same game, or reforming the same nation, or, conceivably, dealing with civilized human beings.

CHAPTER VIII

Conservatives and Private Property

P erhaps no facile political slogan has done more mischief in our time than the pretense that there is a conflict between "human rights and property rights": a
notion popularized in this country by Franklin Roosevelt. All
rights are human rights. Both in point of law and in ethical
theory, beasts, plants, and inanimate objects have no rights.
Only men and women have rights. "Property," as such, enjoys
no rights or privileges; for property is not human. What we
mean by the phrase "property rights" is really the rights of
human beings to possess and acquire property. Property
rights are human rights. They are, indeed, among the most
important of human rights. There is no opposition between
human rights and property rights; if ever a conflict arises, it
is between the human right of owning and acquiring property,
and some other real or pretended human right.

No principle in English and American politics is better
established than respect for the rights of holding and acquiring
private property. Representative government arose out of the
claim of the owners of property that they had a right to be

consulted by the political authority, if their property were to be taxed: this was the origin of popular representation throughout Europe, and the English House of Commons is only the best example of the development of such rights. In America, the principal claim of the Patriots, on the eve of the War of Independence, was that their property was taxed without representation. In America, as in England, nearly everyone was agreed that men and women have three fundamental rights: the right to life, the right to liberty, and the right to property. These three rights were understood to be coordinate and interdependent; for liberty, and even life, could not be secure unless private property was secure. In the Declaration of Independence, the original draft of that document proclaimed that mankind had been endowed naturally with the rights of life, liberty, and property; the phrase "the pursuit of happiness" was substituted for "property" only in Jefferson's revision of the Declaration, and was meant to broaden, rather than to deny, the prescriptive rights of property-holding.

So, the rights of property are ancient and essential human rights. Unless property is secure, there can be no civilized life; for without the right to keep what is one's own, and to add to that if possible, there can be no leisure, no material improvement, no culture worthy of the name. In a condition of anarchy, when every person's property is at the mercy of any strong and ruthless depredator, men and women become so many Cains, their hands against every man's, and every man's against theirs. Bare life, and even a rude form of liberty, may sometimes be possible in a state of anarchy; but they are possible only while men and women live in a savage state. The existence of property, above the most meagre personal possessions, is possible only when some form of political order ensures that a man may keep what is his own. Even savages, indeed, recognize the rights of property in one rudimentary form or another. One of the few points upon which nearly all political theorists have been agreed, in nearly all ages, is that government was created in order to protect the rights of property: Hobbes and Locke, Rousseau and John Adams, are at one here.

"Property is theft," said the anarchist Proudhon. No serious student of society, however, would agree with him; and, for that matter, scarcely any twentieth-century radicals maintain that property, as such, is baneful. The radicals do not wish to abolish property; their aim, rather, is to transfer property from private possessors to state or collective ownership. If property did not exist, civilized life could not exist; and if property exists, someone must own, control, protect, and increase that property. The radical says that property should be owned, controlled, protected, and increased by some collective body—in modern times, ordinarily, by the central political authority. The conservative says that property should be owned, controlled, protected, and increased by private persons and by voluntary associations.

At the dawn of social existence, most property was controlled not by individuals, but by the community; by the little village or tribe or clan. In some parts of the world, ancient collective forms of ownership still survive; and where these primitive institutions remain, the conservative is slow to disturb them, lest he break down the old ways of simple people without providing any adequate substitute for their customs and usages. But in our Western world, and in most civilized societies generally, private property has supplanted collective ownership in proportion as men and women have grown more truly civilized and as those societies have progressed culturally and materially.

Private property has not been an evil that afflicts sophisticated peoples: on the contrary, it has been a great good. Sir Henry Maine, in his *Village Communities,* remarks, "Nobody is at liberty to attack several property and to say at the same time that he values civilization. The history of the two cannot be disentangled." For the institution of several property—that is, private property—has been one of the most powerful instruments for teaching men and women responsibility, for providing motives to integrity, for supporting religion and general culture, for raising mankind above the level of the simple drudge, for giving us leisure to think and freedom to act with moderation and prudence. To be able to keep the fruits of one's labor; to be able to see one's work made permanent; to be able to bequeath one's property to one's posterity; to be able to rise from the natural condition of grinding poverty to the security of enduring accomplishment; to have something that is really one's own—these advantages persuaded men and women to give up the primitive institution of communal property for the civilized institution of private property. The existence of private property means that some men and women will be richer than others, it is true; but if there were no private property, we should not all be rich together: instead, we should all be poor together. Communal holding of property is the mark of poor societies in which there is little property and less progress. "Unless we are willing to pronounce civilization a grand mistake," Paul Elmer More writes, "...unless our material progress is all a grand mistake, we must admit, sadly or cheerfully, that any attempt by government or institution to ignore that inequality, may stop the wheels of progress or throw the world back into temporary barbarism, but will surely not be the cause of wider and greater happiness."

The institution of private property is rooted in inequality; but men, though equal morally, are unequal in every other respect; and to attempt to make them equal by destroying private ownership would only injure the stronger and more energetic natures among men and women without helping the weaker and less provident natures.

Private property, properly understood and properly employed, is not the cause of a gross materialism in society. Quite the contrary: for the modern state in which private property (with insignificant exceptions) has been abolished, Soviet Russia, is the most thoroughly materialistic of all societies that ever have existed, and is proud of her materialism. The civilizations which have been conspicuous for spiritual and intellectual attainment, in ancient and modern times, have been marked by a strong attachment to private property. "One shudders to think of the bleak pall of anxiety and the rage of internecine materialism that would fall upon society," More continues (and Paul Elmer More, one of the most truly civilized of Americans, was an austere moralist and a devout Christian thinker), "were the laws so altered as to transfer the predominant rights from property acquired to the labour by which it is produced. For *if property is secure, it may be the means to an end, whereas if it is insecure it will be the end itself.*" With More, the thinking conservative values property not merely for its own sake, but even more for the sake of the culture and the high civil social order which private property nurtures. Private property never was more secure than in Victorian England: and, whatever the shortcomings of that society, it was a society of the highest moral and intellectual and material accomplishment. Private property rarely was less secure than in Soviet Russia: and there are few sane men and women left today who will attempt to defend Communist culture. Leisure, the basis of culture, flourishes in a society attached to private property; but leisure is denounced in a society dedicated to materialism, like that of the Soviets. The Communists destroy private property, with all its rights and obligations; but they substitute a pursuit of materialism more intense than the love of wealth ascribed to "capitalistic" (that is, private-property-owning) economies.

One of the principal arguments of the modern collectivists has been that if mankind should abolish private property, it would abolish oppression, inequality, and injustice; indeed, the collectivists have maintained that this reform would abolish sin, assuming that sin grows out of private possession and economic inequality. But when they have come to power, the collectivistic theories have been confronted with the uncomfortable fact that no society can exist without property, and that some particular persons, in either a free society or a collectivistic society, must govern that property and allocate its distribution.

In a free society, that property is controlled by a multitude of individuals, no one of whom is powerful enough to inflict his will upon the majority of his fellows. Some of the owners of property are energetic self-made men; others are the custodians of inherited wealth; others are humble and obscure possessors of a house, a little business, a few shares of stock. And this variety makes a society interesting, and ensures a beneficent competition, and prevents any body of squalid oligarchs from dictating to the mass of men and women. In a collectivistic society, on the other hand, that property is controlled by little knots of managers, commissars, far more powerful, and ordinarily far less scrupulous, than any private millionaire. Property has not ceased to be; it has merely changed hands; and the collectivistic domination is less mild, and far less equalitarian, than the old domination of private ownership. Private property, in short, is essential to freedom. Men and women must eat. If they are economically dependent upon a single master, they are slaves. In the collectivistic domination, the state is that single master, and the state will not abide dissent. In the name of equality, the collectivist establishes a political and economic order which subjects a great mass of impotent individuals to the will and whim of a new managerial elite. So long as private property survives in a healthy condition, this collectivistic domination cannot be established. But when private ownership of property has been abolished, it is nearly impossible to maintain the least resistance to tyranny. Private property is, to some extent, an end in itself; but it is also a means to culture; and it is a means to freedom.

Now if the conservative does not hesitate to assert the positive rights of private property, neither is he slow to acknowledge that property has its responsibilities. With Ruskin, he declares, "Whereas it has long been known and declared that the poor have no right to the property of the rich, I wish it also to be known and declared that the rich have no right to the property of the poor." The conservative believes that the private conscience, the courts, and the government should be always vigilant to protect the rights of every person and class. It is not wealth as such that the conservative respects, but the rights of property, large and small. Most persons' property-holdings are small. Without these small holdings, all large holdings would be in peril. Economic consolidation, monopoly, and what may be called "private collectivism" are suspect to the conservative. The rich man has rights not because he is rich, but because he is a man; and in protecting his wealth, we protect the smaller possessions of all men and women.

Yes, property has its duties. In the Christian view, property is bestowed upon particular persons that they may serve God and their fellow-men by putting property to good use. The men and women who possess property have the moral duties of charity, prudence, and frugality. And, possession always encouraging our natural tendencies toward pride, presumption, indifference, and sloth, the possessors of wealth in every generation need to be reminded of the duty of using their property generously and charitably. The state sometimes must act to restrain the arrogant wealthy, just as sometimes it must act to restrain the covetous poor. But it is Providence, together with private energies, that has created property. The state did not create property; instead, the state is the constituted guardian of property. When the state abandons its role of protector and assumes a role for which it was not intended—the role of master and allocator of property—then the conservative strives to confine the political authority within its proper limits. The state, he thinks, is entitled to interfere with established rights of property only in times of great emergency, and then only for what is an unquestioned general good. By appeal to individual consciences and public opinion, rather than to political authority, the conservative seeks to remind the possessors of property of their natural duties, as well as their natural rights.

CHAPTER IX

Conservatives and Power

S carcely any political aphorism is more widely quoted today than Lord Acton's observation that "power tends to corrupt, and absolute power corrupts absolutely"; yet the barriers against concentration of power—political power and economic power—are steadily reduced in our age, throughout almost all the world, with little effectual protest. The conservative, intent upon preserving order and justice and freedom, does what he can to remind the modern world of the truth of Acton's statement, and to retain those checks upon arbitrary power which distinguish a free society from a servile society.

The American War of Independence was the result of the colonists' protest that Parliament was usurping to itself powers anciently reserved to the several colonies. The *Federalist Papers*, which are the chief American contribution to the literature of politics, are permeated with the conviction that power must be hedged, limited, reserved, kept in balance. The Federal Constitution, in essence, is an instrument for checking and balancing political power: the powers of federal and state governments, the powers of political authority and of private citizens, the powers of executive and legislative and judiciary. The practical understanding of the problem of power that was manifested by American statesmen like John Adams and James Madison has left its mark upon our institutions to this day.

Power, politically speaking, is the ability to do as one likes, regardless of the wills of one's fellows and neighbors. A state in which an individual or a small group are able to dominate the wills of their fellows without check is a despotism, whether it is called "monarchical" or "aristocratic" or "democratic." When every person claims to be a power unto himself, then a society is in anarchy. Anarchy never lasts long, being intolerable to everyone, and contrary to the inescapable fact that some persons are stronger and cleverer than their neighbors. To anarchy there always succeeds tyranny or oligarchy, in which power is monopolized by a very few. The conservative endeavors so to limit and balance political power that anarchy or tyranny cannot arise. But men and women, in every age, are tempted to disregard the limitations upon power for the sake of some fancied temporary advantage. It is characteristic of the radical that he thinks of power as a force for good—so long as the power falls into his hands. In the name of liberty, the French and Russian revolutionaries abolished the old restrictions upon power; but power cannot be abolished; it always finds its way into someone's control; and, in France at the end of the eighteenth century and in Russia at the beginning of the twentieth century, the power which the revolutionaries had thought oppressive in the hands of the old regime became many times as tyrannical in the hands of the radical new masters of the state, who had stripped away what checks upon power the French and Russian monarchies never had dared to tamper with.

In some degree, nearly all men and women desire power; and with some persons, the desire for power is an overweening lust. No passion is more powerful than this. It is one of the errors of Marxism to exaggerate the importance of the economic motive in society. Most men and women, indeed, do desire material possessions. But many persons are much fonder of power than they are of wealth. One of the chief reasons for the acquiring of wealth, for that matter, is that wealth often means power. The conservative, looking upon human nature as a mixture of good and evil, capable sometimes of high nobility, yet always in some sense flawed, knows that the thirst for power among us never will be quenched. No matter how prosperous or how nearly equal men and women are, they always will seek power. Accepting that sorry fact, the conservative seeks to set bounds to this power-appetite by ethical instruction and by good laws.

If only private property were abolished, some radical reformers have insisted, then mankind would be happy: because property, they have contended, is the root of all evil. If only social privilege were abolished, other radical reformers have declared, then mankind would be emancipated from envy and unjust ambition; because privilege, they have thought, is the source of man's inhumanity to man. These notions tended to dominate the liberal era of the past century and a half, and they are influential among us still. But they are fallacies. Property is sought by the unscrupulous not so much for its own sake as for the sake of the power which property generally confers. Privilege is sought by the unscrupulous much more for the sake of the power which it veils than for the sake of mere ostentation. If property and privilege and all the old motives to integrity and incentives to diligence which have been the characteristics of Western civilization were abolished tomorrow, still the fierce disagreement between man and man would continue; indeed, it probably would rage still more fiercely; for when only power remains as a gratification to ambition, then power will be the more ardently desired and the more ruthlessly pursued. And no one, I repeat, ever succeeds in abolishing power. Like energy, power is not dissipated; it merely changes forms.

In that terrible novel *1984*, George Orwell describes a society, merely a generation distant from our era, in which the only remaining gratification for the stronger and more talented natures is the possession of power. Religion is gone; privilege, in the old sense, is gone; private property is gone; liberal learning is gone; family life is gone; art is gone; philosophy is gone; simple contentment is gone. But there remains one ferocious motive to success, the lust after power. One sensation, in this society, still is pleasurable: the sensation of stamping forever on a human face. And the masters of this society so thoroughly enjoy this sensation that they consider it more than sufficient compensation for all that has been lost.

This is the triumph of a diabolical impulse, the ascendancy of Pride, the indulgence of that will to dominate one's fellows which Christian teaching always has endeavored to subdue. But Orwell's picture is not fantastic. We have seen within the past forty years the realization of this horrid regime in a great part of the world. A Socialist member of Parliament, returned from a visit to Poland, recently declared that he had seen in Soviet Poland the literal fulfillment of Orwell's fantasy. All the old checks on power had been abolished, together with all the old motives to integrity; and the consequence was a society by the side of which the most despotic government of the eighteenth century was gently liberal. All the humanitarian slogans of the Communists were of no weight when tossed into the balance against naked power.

Among a people who, like the Americans, have long been accustomed to a habitual and almost unconscious restraining and balancing of power—so long accustomed that they have nearly forgotten that such checks and balances exist—there is a perilous tendency to neglect the grim problem of power. Good will, economic reforms, and liberal slogans can remedy all the ills to which flesh is heir, the doctrinaire liberal argues; and many Americans, protected by national usage and sound constitutions from the more extreme risks of the pursuit of power, accept these arguments with little question. Thus, for instance, our foreign policy tends to degenerate into mere economic generosity—appropriation after appropriation for material assistance to "underdeveloped countries," or well-meant advice, accompanied by technical aid, to the leaders of Asia and Africa that if only they will struggle upward toward the American standard of living, internal disorder and international hostility will give way to the good society.

Now there are instances in which material assistance to other nations can achieve considerable benefits. But to assume that mere economic reform, of itself, can give peace to the nations is to ignore the whole ancient problem of power. And that problem, soon or late, refuses to be ignored. For economic gain is not the principal desire of most statesmen or of most nations. Prestige, glory, and especially power are more powerful motives. Among the nations which are reasonably prosperous, a sacrifice of some prosperity for a great deal of power often seems well worthwhile: thus, Hitler successfully exhorted the Germans to exchange butter for guns. Among the nations which are deeply sunk in poverty, the possibility of any real and lasting improvement of their material condition is so remote that often they eagerly abandon this tiring struggle for the exciting pursuit of power.

In this, the Soviets have shown themselves cleverer than we. For though the Communists profess "dialectical materialism" and material aggrandizement for the masses, in reality the masters of Soviet Russia play always the great grim game of power; their desire is domination, not universal prosperity; and they know how to play upon this ancient appetite for mastery over men and women. We promise ten times as much in economic assistance to the "underdeveloped countries" as the Russians do; we deliver a hundred times as much such assistance; and yet we have not been notably successful in our contest against Communist intrigue in Asia and Africa. For the Russians have played the game of power, while we have innocently practiced the materialism that the Russians preach. And, the desire for power being stronger than the desire for wealth among energetic men and women, the Soviets have touched chords in human nature which we Americans have neglected.

Now the conservative of reflection does not recommend that we ought to model our conduct upon successful Soviet intrigues. He does not believe that the unscrupulous encouragement of the appetite for power is a legitimate tactic of national interest. But he does realize that we cannot afford to leave out of our calculations, in foreign policy or in domestic, the ancient inclinations of the human heart. Men and women desire prestige, glory, power: very well, accept that fact, and try to direct that longing into ways of justice and order and freedom. Power, properly guarded and limited and channeled, is the means by which all improvement is undertaken. In itself, power is neither moral nor immoral: everything depends on the motives with which power is employed and the institutions which check its abuse. To treat other nations as if their only desires were material is to insult them grossly; even while accepting our assistance, under such circumstances, they will resent our presumption; and they will employ our assistance to play their own game of power. Justly checked and balanced power is respected and admired; unchecked and unscrupulous exercise of power is dreaded and envied; but neglected power is despised. These considerations, the conservative believes, ought to influence our foreign policy.

And our domestic policy ought also to be governed by a true apprehension of the nature of power. Men and women are not naturally good. Good and evil, rather, are intricately interwoven in their natures; and when the good predominates, it ordinarily is by virtue of emulation, habit, and obedience to just laws. If the old decencies, customs, and laws are swept away—no matter how generously humanitarian the excuse—the precarious balance of good over evil may be upset, and the old lust after power is released to work its old corruption. Constitutional restrictions, states' rights, local self-government, limitation upon executive authority, strict interpretation of the laws: all these devices to hedge and balance power often seem annoyingly old-fangled, particularly in an age of rapid economic expansion. The impulse of the doctrinaire liberal is to sweep away these barriers to reform.

But human nature also is annoyingly old-fangled; and when the usages and the constitutional provisions that have sheltered order and justice and freedom among us these three centuries are disregarded, all sorts of disagreeable problems, scarcely anticipated by the liberal doctrinaire, spring up among us. The problem of fixing responsibility in the giant union; the problem of fixing responsibility in the giant corporation; the difficulty of reconciling planning on a grand scale with the fallibility of any single human intellect—these, and many more such conundrums, are closely related to the human appetite for power and to the conservative principle that it is better not to do a thing at all than to do it by means which may imperil the whole complex civil social order. Order, justice, and freedom are not products of nature; on the contrary, they are most artificial and elaborate human contrivances, developed slowly and painfully out of the experience of many generations of men and women. Order, justice, and freedom cannot abide the general release of power from its ancient shackles. It may be hard to have at one's elbow the energy that could make the world anew and not to use it; but it is harder still, that power released, to restore the tolerable balance of influences which we call a free society.

CHAPTER X

Conservatives and Education

For the reflecting conservative, the purpose of education is clear. That purpose is to develop the mental and moral faculties of the individual person, for the person's own sake. Now this process of cultivating the mind and conscience of young people (here I speak of education in the sense of "schooling," though it is quite true that self-education ought to continue most of any man's or woman's life) has certain lesser purposes and incidental benefits. One of these lesser aims is to instruct young people in the beliefs and customs which make possible a decent civil social order. Another of these lesser aims is the inculcation of certain skills and aptitudes which will help young people as they come to man's estate. Yet another is the development of habits of sociability—teaching boys and girls how to take a normal part in society. And there are more purposes and benefits.

Yet the conservative does not forget that the *essential* aim, and the chief benefit, of formal education is to make people intelligent and good. Schools cannot, wholly by themselves, make people intelligent and good; natural inclinations or disinclinations, the family, and the community have a great deal to do with whether young people are wise or foolish, good or bad. But schools can help in the process. And if schools neglect this primary function in favor of vague schemes for "group play" or "personality unfolding" or "learning by doing" or "adjustment to the group" or "acquiring approved social attitudes," then they have become bad schools.

The conservative always thinks first of the individual human person. What is bad for individuals cannot be good for society. And if most individual men and women are reasonably good and reasonably intelligent, the society in which they live cannot become a very bad one. Therefore—especially in this time which Ortega y Gasset calls "the mass-age," this time in which standardization and various forms of collectivism threaten the whole concept of true individual personality—the conservative never ceases to emphasize that the school exists primarily to help improve the understanding and the moral worth of private persons. The school is not merely a custodial institution, to keep young people in a tolerable captivity while their parents are busy elsewhere. It is not merely a place where young people are taught how to make money in years to come. It is not merely a means for indoctrinating young people in certain approved social attitudes. No, it is something much more important: it is an institution for imparting a sound intellectual and moral discipline to the rising generation. The conservative is not afraid of the abused word "discipline." Without discipline, men and women must spend their lives either in mischief or in idleness. The best form of discipline is self-discipline; and self-discipline, mental and ethical, is what the schools try to impart to students.

But to the modern radical who is faithful to his own first principles, formal education is something quite different from what the conservative thinks education should be. To the radical—communist, or fascist, or socialist, or any sort of radical ideologue—the school is an instrument of power. It is a means for indoctrinating the young with what the radical believes to be the concept of the good society. The school, in the radical's opinion, exists to serve "society," not primarily to serve the individual human person. And the scholar, in the radical's opinion, ought not to waste his time searching fo Truth: instead, he ought to be preaching approved social doctrines to the young, or in advancing the class struggle, or in planning for a better world. The radical thinks of the school as a means for improving, or at least changing, society in the mass. To the modern radical, the very idea of encouraging the development of private talents merely for the sake of private character is annoying. He thinks of the school as a means of advancing toward some form of collectivism. He cannot see the trees for the forest. The private person, and the private person's reason, are very little to him; the amorphous masses are everything.

Now of course there are persons of radical political views among us today who do not embrace the radical theory of education that I have suggested above. But these are inconsistent radicals, just as there are inconsistent conservatives. If the only real object of life is the material betterment of the masses, presumably to be accomplished through the establishment of equality of condition, then there is no point in encouraging development of strong private opinions and strong individual minds. What collectivism requires is not strong personalities and a high degree of private culture, but rather unquestioning conformity to the secular dogmas of collectivism. The more consistent and forthright radical educators, like Professor Theodore Brameld, confess this truth and urge us to convert the schools into propaganda devices for teaching the doctrines that "everybody belongs to everybody else" and that one person is as good as another, or maybe a little better. Quite candidly, they call themselves Social Reconstructionists—educators who would employ the schools to build a new collectivistic society. They intend to break down all the old beliefs and loyalties, through the process of educating the young, and to supplant these old beliefs and loyalties with artificially cultivated attachment to collectivistic doctrines. Some of them would teach "the religion of democracy," to replace the religious convictions in which nearly all schools had their origins. They do not want reverent or inquiring minds; they desire only submissive and uniform minds.

When such theories as these are baldly presented to the American public, that public promptly rejects them. But what the American public has not yet rejected is something more subtle, less candid, and—in the long run—perhaps as dangerous: the educational notions of the late John Dewey. Sound sense and fallacy are blended in Dewey's theories, but the fallacies have become almost official educational dogma in our country, while the sound sense either has been forgotten or has lost its significance because of altered social circumstances. Dewey desired the state schools to become a means for making the American population homogeneous. Hostile toward traditional religion (though sometimes giving it lip-service of sorts), he hoped that a thoroughgoing and aggressive secularism in the schools would take the place of the religious concepts which have been the foundation of American morals and politics. Hostile toward the works of the higher imagination, he proposed to substitute "group endeavor" and "learning by doing" for the literary studies and intellectual disciplines which had given American education its established character.

Dewey's theories and influence cannot be examined in detail here; they have been intelligently criticized in recent years by Canon Bernard Iddings Bell, Professor Arthur Bestor, Mr. Mortimer Smith, Mr. Albert Lynd, Dr. Gordon Keith Chalmers, and others. What I am trying to do is to suggest the attitude toward formal education which the intelligent conservative ought to take. The intelligent conservative combines a disposition to preserve with an ability to reform. And our schools need reform most pressingly. Despite all the talk about "education for democracy," they seem to be educating for mass-submission; dreary secular indoctrination is substituted for the inquiring mind. The Republic cannot long survive if its citizens are incapable of apprehending general ideas, or even of reading and writing; and the failure of our schools—and, to a considerable extent, of our universities and colleges—has brought us to just that pass. Many college graduates today cannot write a simple letter as well as a sixth-grade student would have written it fifty years ago.

So the conservative believes that we ought to say less about "group dynamics" and "social reconstruction" in our schools, and do more to restore the old and indispensable disciplines of reading, writing, mathematics, the sciences, imaginative literature, and history. He thinks that we need to bring back definite "subject-matter" courses and abolish vague catch-ails like "social studies" (taught as a single amorphous course) and "communications." He thinks that our colleges and universities could profit greatly by a return to humane learning—to the real humanities, those disciplines designed to teach ethical understanding and develop the higher imagination; they ought to redeem themselves from an excessive vocationalism, from a mistaken eagerness to attract students which gives everyone a degree but no one an education, and from a false specialization. Alfred North Whitehead remarked once that the ancient philosopher aspired to teach wisdom, but that the modern professor aspires only to teach facts. Isolated facts, the conservative thinks, do not constitute an education; and vague sentiments and "approved social attitudes" have still less to do with the true educational process. For what the Republic requires is a citizenry endowed with a knowledge of the wisdom of our ancestors, and a respect for that wisdom; a citizenry endowed with the ability to form opinions and make judgments. And what the truly human person requires is a grasp of those genuine disciplines of the mind which make it possible for him to become, in the full sense, a reasoning being. An "educational" system which does less than this is not educational at all, but only a propaganda-apparatus in the service of the state.

With the medieval schoolmen, the conservative is of the opinion that we moderns are dwarfs standing upon the shoulders of giants—able to see further than our intellectual ancestors only because we are supported by the great bulk and strength of their achievement. If we spurn the wisdom of our ancestors, we tumble down into the ditch of ignorance. Lacking the old disciplines which inculcated ethical principles and encouraged the ordered imagination, any people sink into a cultural decline; and they are liable to become the victims of any clever clique of unprincipled manipulators.

Yet, despite all these faults in twentieth-century American education, the conservative knows that our system possesses still some considerable merits. Conspicuous among those virtues is the diversity and competition surviving among our educational institutions. We have not merely state schools, but a large number of private and church-supported schools; and the conservative approves this healthy variety. Disciples of Dewey like Dr. James Conant urge us to sweep away private and parochial establishments and force the whole population into a common mode of schooling, completely secularized and intended to "teach democracy." The conservative sets his face against such arrogant proposals. On the contrary, he thinks we are fortunate in escaping the deadening influence of uniformity in the educational process. He is glad that we have not merely state universities, but old endowed private universities of high reputation, hundreds of private and church-sponsored colleges, opportunity for experiment, and freedom of choice among professors and students. If a nation desires intellectual vitality and originality, it will encourage this variety; if it is resigned to stagnation and secular conformity, however, a nation will embrace the uniformity-designs of Dewey and Conant.

Centralization of any sort is suspect to the conservative; and centralization of the educational establishment is one of the most dangerous forms of centralization. It is with marked hostility, then, that the conservative looks upon proposals for federal subsidies to the public schools. The man who pays the fiddler calls the tune, the conservative knows; and, besides, education is more vigorous when it is supported by local endeavor. The only very valuable piece of information to come out of the White House Conference on Education, in 1955, was the conclusion that no state in the Union is unable to bear its own educational responsibilities. Private citizens, local communities, and the several states, the conservative knows, are the best judges of their own educational needs and interests. When he is approached with proposals for consolidation and unification, he shrewdly suspects that somewhere in the dim background of these proposals is someone's Grand Design for employing the schools as a tool for turning society inside out. And the conservative has no intention of turning society inside out. He thinks that to abuse the schools for such a purpose would be to corrupt education. The natural function of formal education is conservative, in the best sense of that word: that is, formal education conserves the best of what has been thought and written and discovered in the past, and by a regular discipline teaches us to guide ourselves by the light of the wisdom of our ancestors.

A Scottish friend of mine writes to me of the confused notions that curse our age: "People seem to accept premises that have been rejected by the wise through all the ages, and there is a horrible ominous throbbing in the air like the sound of countless trotters on the cliff-head at Gadara." All the good places and people, he continues, are being sacrificed "not to a candid malevolence but to unbearably specious cant." Unbearably specious cant characterizes much of what passes for education among us nowadays. One of the works of conservative reform most urgently needed is a return to right reason, a restoration of honorable disciplines in education. And the first step in this reform must be a recognition of the enduring principle that education is intended for the elevation of the mind and conscience of the individual human person. It is not intended to be a toy for radical doctrinaires to play with, nor yet to be a great sham affording profit and prestige to what Mr. David Riesman calls "the patronage network of Teachers' College, Columbia University." The conservative respects the works of the mind; the radical, in our age, seems to be smugly content with cant and slogan.

Chapter XI

Permanence and Change

The liveliest definition of a conservative is Ambrose Bierce's in his *Devil's Dictionary*: "Conservative, n. A statesman who is enamored of existing evils, as distinguished from the Liberal, who wishes to replace them with others." The conservative, truly, represents the feeling of sympathy with the past, the forces of permanence in society; the liberal, the feeling of glory in the future, the forces of change in society. Since it is the liberal who desires radical alteration of the existing order, ordinarily the liberal is more active than the conservative. It is the liberal, ordinarily, who writes polemical tracts and organizes mass movements; the conservative, except when he is aroused by dread of radical change or alarmed by the decay of his society, tends to rely upon the powerful and stable forces of custom and habit. It is this tendency which gave John Stuart Mill an excuse for calling conservatives "the stupid party." Thus, Lord Silverbridge, in Trollope's novel *The Duke's Children*, tells his father the Duke of Omnium, by way of apology for having joined the Conservative Party: "In comparison with a great many men, I know that I am a fool. Perhaps it is because I know that, that I am a Conservative. The Radicals are always saying that a Conservative must be a fool. Then a fool ought to be a Conservative."

Yet when the reflecting conservative is roused to serious thought and action, often he can move with a power startling to his radical or liberal adversaries. Cicero in the time of the dissolution of the Roman Republic, Falkland in the English Civil Wars, Burke in the age of the French Revolution, and John Adams in the early years of our Republic are examples of this power. And nowadays American conservatives, roused to the dread threat of the totalist state, are writing and acting to some purpose.

There are stupid conservatives, just as there are stupid liberals and radicals; but conservatives really are not the "stupid party." It has been said that "conservatism is enjoyment." The conservative believes life, despite all its afflictions, to be good; and he believes our American society, despite all its defects, to be sound at the core. Therefore, enjoying life and our old institutions, he does not share the radical's frantic desire to mould all things anew. He does not believe that ours is the worst of all possible worlds; and he does not believe that there ever will be a perfect world, here below. Conservatives are the stupid party only in the sense that radicals are the neurotic party: that is, if some conservatives are merely dull and complacent, nevertheless some radicals are merely hysterical and malcontent—the men who went out to David in the Cave of Adullam. "Ordinarily," the late Professor F. J. C. Hearnshaw wrote once, "it is sufficient merely for the conservative to sit and think, or perhaps merely to sit."

Burke compared the conservative English of his day to great cattle browsing under the English oaks, silent and seemingly stupid when compared with the myriads of radical grasshoppers chirping in the meadow round about them; but when real strength is in question, he added, the grasshoppers are as nothing by the side of the conservative cattle. It is so still. A large number of conservatives now realize that it will not suffice for them merely to sit; they must think as well, and act; and I think that they may act to some purpose.

Stupidity is one of the principal accusations against conservatives—though what is meant by it, ordinarily, is simply that conservatives do not believe that abstract schemes of positive law and mass-meetings can make this world of ours into a terrestrial paradise. Another charge frequently brought against conservatives is that they oppose Progress. And this latter charge has just as much foundation as the former: that is, some superficial justification for it exists; but when one examines the real first principles of conservatism, one finds that the thinking conservative is grossly misinterpreted by his radical critics.

The conservative is not opposed to progress as such, though he doubts very much that there is any such force as a mystical Progress, with a Roman P, at work in the world. When a society is progressing in some respects, usually it is declining in other respects. The conservative knows that any healthy society contains two elements, what Coleridge called its Permanence and its Progression.

The Permanence in a society is formed by those enduring values and interests which give us stability and continuity;

without that Permanence, the fountains of the great deep are broken up, and society slips into anarchy. The Progression in a society is that spirit and that body of talents which urge us on to prudent reform and improvement; without that Progression, a people stagnate, and society subsides into an Egyptian or a Peruvian lethargy. The intelligent conservative, therefore, endeavors to reconcile the claims of Permanence and the claims of Progression. He thinks that the liberal and the radical, blind to the just claims of Permanence, would endanger all the great heritage bequeathed to us by our ancestors in a rash endeavor to bestow upon us a dubious future of alleged universal happiness. The conservative, in short, is in favor of reasoned and temperate progress; he is opposed to the abstract cult of Progress, which cult assumes that everything new is necessarily better than everything old.

Change is essential to a good society, the conservative reasons. Just as the human body uses up old tissue and takes on new, so the body politic must discard, from time to time, some of its old ways and take on certain beneficent innovations. A body that has ceased to renew itself has begun to die. But if that body is to be healthy, the change must be in a regular manner, and harmonious with the form and nature of that body; otherwise, change produces a monstrous growth, a cancer, which devours its host. The conservative takes care that nothing in society should ever be wholly old, and nothing should ever be wholly new. This is the means of the conservation of our society, just as it is the means of conservation of our physical bodies.

Just how much change, however, a society requires, and what sort of change, depend upon the spirit of the age and the peculiar conditions of the society in question. It is one of the faults of the radical that commonly he advocates immediate and perilous change at the very time when gradual and temperate change already has commenced. Thus, it was in the French Revolution: as Tocqueville wrote of his nation, "Halfway down the stairs, we threw ourselves out of the window in order to get to the ground more quickly." The conservative believes that any change which means a sharp break with established interests and usages is perilous; and he maintains that change, if it is to achieve real benefits, must be the voluntary work of many individuals and associations, not decreed by some presumptuous central authority. The United States have altered greatly since the founding of the Republic; some of those changes have been for good, and some for ill; but it is one of the chief merits of our country that we have not been in love with change for the mere sake of change. Our prosperity and comparative tranquility are the result, in no small measure, of the fact that we always have tried to reconcile the best in the old order with the improvements which our ingenuity has suggested. And our change has been the work, not of someone's Grand Design, but of the independent endeavors of many men and women working prudently.

Some very important things, however, the conservative knows to be immutable; and he holds that it is highly dangerous to tamper with that which probably cannot be altered for the better. He does not think that we can change human nature, in the mass, for the better; there is only one sort of improvement in human nature, and that is internal improvement—the improvement every man and every woman can work privately. He does not think that we can improve upon the Ten Commandments as a guide to virtue. He does not think that we can create out of whole cloth a form of government better suited to our national temper than that which we already have. He holds, in short, that the great discoveries in morals and in politics already have been made; we will do well to employ these truths, rather than to seek vaguely for some new dispensation. He says, as Burke said more than a century and a half ago in reply to the eighteenth-century advocates of a new morality and a new politics, "We know that *we* have made no new discoveries; and we think that no discoveries are to be made, in morality; nor many in the great principles of government, nor in the ideas of liberty, which were understood long before we were born altogether as well as they will be after the grave has heaped its mould upon our presumption, and the silent tomb shall have imposed its law on our pert loquacity."

If one has to choose between the two, Permanence is more important than Progression. Between a custom and an institution that are known to function fairly well, and a custom and an institution that are unknown qualities, it is wiser to prefer the old and tried over the new and untried. Randolph of Roanoke cried out to a startled House of Representatives, "Gentlemen, I have found the philosopher's stone! It is this: never, without the greatest provocation, to disturb a thing that is at rest." The elaborate fabric which we call our civil social order—the complex of moral habits, political establishments, customary laws, and economic ways—has been erected over many centuries by a painful and laborious process of trial and error. It is the product of filtered wisdom, "the democracy of the dead," the considered opinions and the weighed experience of many generations. If we demolish that edifice, it is scarcely possible for us to rebuild it. Our established order works; we cannot be sure that some conjectured new order would work. And we have no right to play with society as if it were a toy; the rights of millions living and more millions yet to be born are at stake here. So, I repeat, whenever a clear choice has to be made, we are wise if we prefer Permanence to Progression.

But often it is not necessary to make that choice. Frequently we have it in our power to combine moderate and measured progress with the present advantages of established society. The prudent conservative does not forget his obligation to unite to a disposition to preserve an ability to reform. The American conservative character has made it possible for us to grow from a few millions of people in Atlantic seaboard colonies to a great nation of a hundred and eighty million, extending from the Arctic to the Caribbean and from bases in Africa to bases in Korea. This has been genuine progress; but it has been progress within the framework of tradition. In accomplishing this progress, we have preserved almost intact the moral and social institutions with which our Republic commenced. Such is the conservative's ideal of the satisfactory relationship between permanence and change. The grand principles endure; it is only their application which alters.

Canon Bernard Iddings Bell, a generation ago—when nearly everyone who wanted to be *a la mode* called himself a liberal—set down as accurate and pitiless a description of modern liberalism as I know:

> A Liberal, to be brief, is one who thinks that human beings are by nature good and trustworthy, and that everything is sure to get better and better by mere lapse of time, provided only that we rid our lives of unfortunate social maladjustments brought about by ancient wickedness such as, of course, no longer exists, and can free human minds from the inhibitions of supernatural religion. The Liberal believes that man is a noble fellow with no soul, and that as such he is sure to come to possess the most sublime creations of culture as a sort of by-product of enlightened self-interest, or, as the vulgar put it, of "keeping an eye on the ball." In education, the liberal regards with awe "the unspoiled human baby," and seeks to develop that baby not by way of teaching him the necessary disciplines, but rather by letting him do as he pleases. In politics, the liberal believes that if you give a vote to every human being and always direct public policy in accordance with the majority of ballots cast, the highest possible social good is inevitably the result.

So much for the liberal. The conservative is a very different sort of being. The conservative knows that he was not born yesterday. He is aware that all the benefits of our complex civilization are the delicate creations of many generations of painstaking and sacrificing effort. It is not "by mere lapse of time" that everything gets better and better; when things improve, it is because conscientious men and women, working within the framework of tradition, have struggled valiantly against evil and sloth. Progress, though too rare in history, is real; but it is the work of artifice, of human ingenuity and prudence; it is not automatic. And progress is possible only so long as it is undertaken upon the sure footing of permanence.

CHAPTER XII

What Is the Republic?

The word "republic" means public things, the commonwealth, the general welfare as expressed in political forms. The idea of the Republic lies at the heart of American conservative thought. We have not known monarchy since 1776, and we always have been suspicious of "pure democracy"—that is, government by the masses, without constitutional checks, protection for minorities, and representative institutions. Our government, as Calhoun said, "is, of course, a Republic, a constitutional democracy, in contradistinction to an absolute democracy; and ... the theory which regards it as a government of the mere numerical majority rests on a gross and groundless misconception."

The aim of the collectivistic state is to abolish classes, voluntary associations, and private rights, swallowing all these in the formless blur of "the general will" and absolute equality of condition—equality, that is, of everyone except the clique which rules the state. The aim of our Republic, on the contrary, has been to reconcile classes, protect voluntary associations, and nourish private rights. We do not recognize any "general will," but only the opinions of private citizens and legitimate groups. We do not seek equality of condition, but only equality of legal rights—the classical principle of justice, "to each his own."

For Americans, the good commonwealth has been the state in which men and women might follow their own bent, subject only to the dictates of morality and the regulations necessary to the administration of justice. We have reserved to private persons a great body of rights. We have conferred upon local and state governments only such powers as are necessary for keeping order and undertaking duties that no individual or voluntary association can perform. We have delegated to our federal government only certain explicit powers, dealing with matters beyond the general competence of the states. And though this original arrangement of rights and powers has been altered in some degree since the founding of our Republic, in general these theories of right and responsibility still prevail among us, and we continue to believe that the just Republic is a commonwealth in which as many things as possible are left to private and local management; and in which the state, far from obliterating classes and voluntary associations and private rights, shelters and respects all these.

We never have fallen, most of us, into the error that "commonwealth" means "collectivism." Our common freedom and our common prosperity have been nurtured, one may say, by a salutary neglect of the notion of an absolute central sovereignty. This original conservative cast of our politics has not departed from among us. We have not been enchanted by the fallacy that the will of the majority is the will of God: for us, on the contrary, the successful Republic is marked by sound security against the will and appetite of temporary and unthinking majorities.

Our Republic, in short, has been a complex of private and local liberties. Its great merit has been not equality, but freedom. Yet there are signs that public affection for this Republic, and understanding of it, are diminishing in our day. Sometimes we seem nearly to have arrived at the condition in which Cicero found the Roman Republic in his time. He describes that crumbling commonwealth in his treatise called *The Republic:*

> Long before our own time, the customs of our ancestors moulded admirable men, and in turn these eminent men upheld the ways and institutions of their forebears. Our age, however, inherited the Republic like some beautiful painting of bygone days, its colors already fading through great age; and not only has our generation neglected to freshen the colors of the picture, but we have failed to preserve its form and outlines. For what remains to us, nowadays, of the ancient ways on which the commonwealth, they tell us, was founded? We see them so lost in oblivion that they are not merely neglected, but quite forgot. And what am I to say of the men? Our customs have perished for want of men to stand by them, and now we are called to an accounting, so that we stand impeached like men accused of capital crimes, compelled to plead our own cause.

Through our vices, rather than from chance, we
retain the word "republic" long after we have lost
the reality.

Lest we Americans, too, retain only the word "republic"
but not the reality, we need to undertake the conservative task
of restoring in our generation an understanding of that freedom and that order which have expressed and encouraged our
national genius. This has been one of the principal ends of my
little book.

When many people use the word "freedom" nowadays,
they use it in the sense of the French revolutionaries: freedom
from tradition, from established social institutions, from religious beliefs, from prescriptive duties. But this is not the sense
in which the founders of our Republic understood freedom.
For them, freedom and order were not at opposite poles;
instead, they knew that one cannot possibly have enduring
freedom without order, and that there can be no really just
order without a high degree of private freedom. It is this
apprehension of freedom which we must refresh, if our Republic is to endure.

The conservative endeavors to conserve certain great and
ancient things. He endeavors to conserve the religious and
moral traditions that make us more than beasts. He endeavors
to conserve the legacy of Western civilization, the wisdom of
our ancestors, that makes us more than barbarians. And he
endeavors to conserve that civil social order, political and economic, which has been developed through the experience and
trials of so many generations, and which confers upon us a

tolerable measure of justice and order and freedom. In the present age, the conservative is particularly zealous to conserve freedom. We stand in no immediate peril of material want or of anarchy. But we are in danger, almost imminently, of a loss of freedom that would make us less than truly human. Therefore, the modern conservative tends to emphasize the claims of liberty, although in another age he might need to emphasize the claims of charity and duty. But, if he is true to his own principles, he does not forget that every freedom is married to a responsibility.

In my previous chapters, I have said little enough about political economy, principally because I think that economics has been over-emphasized in our generation. I do not believe that the great contest in the modern world is simply between two theories of economics, "socialism" and "capitalism," as Bernard Shaw tried to convince women a generation ago. No, I happen to think that the real struggle is between *traditional society*, with its religious and moral and political inheritance, and *collectivism* (under whatever name) with its passion for reducing humanity to a mere tapioca-pudding of identical producers and consumers. There is far more to this struggle, in short, than questions of profits and wages and management. But nowadays we are menaced by an economic collectivism which, if triumphant among us, would put an end not merely to a free economy, but to freedom of every description. Therefore, I think it worthwhile to write a little about the necessities of economic freedom.

Without a free economy, freedom of any sort is most difficult to maintain. The Republic is more important than any especial economic system; yet the Republic cannot endure without an economy substantially free. There are two principal reasons why—given the conditions of modern America, and the political institutions that are ours—a free economy is essential to the preservation of freedom in general: to intellectual freedom, to civil liberties, to representative government, to freedom of private character. The first of these is that men and women can enjoy external freedom only if they are subject to no single, absolute master for their subsistence. The second of these is that ordinary integrity requires ordinary rewards, and that in a collectivistic economy (whether called "capitalistic" or "communistic" or "socialistic," or what you will) the old motives to integrity, the ancient reasons for responsible conduct, are lacking.

First, a few words about the former reason. Men and women must eat. If they are dependent upon a solitary power or a solitary individual for their subsistence, they are slaves. They can act in any external respect only upon the sufferance of that master. If that master is the state, they have no alternative employment; they must obey, or live on air; and the state, because of its impersonality, can be a harder master, more devoid of charity and generosity, than any medieval lord.

To say that the "democratic" state would not deprive anyone of liberty is to play upon words. The democratic state, like any other, is directed by individuals, with all the failings to which humanity is heir, especially the failing of the lust for power. To suppose that the mass-state would be always just and generous toward its slaves is to suppose that there would exist, upon all its levels, a class of philosopher-kings superior to human frailty, purged of lust and envy and petty ambition. But in modern America we have no such class to draw upon; indeed, often we seem to be doing what we can to abolish that sense of inherent responsibility and high honor which compensates a patriarchal or feudal society for its lack of private liberty. It is more probable, as George Santayana suggests, that we would be the subjects of a host of squalid oligarchs, devoid of the high sense of responsibility. The Republic would have perished.

And a few words about the second reason. Most people do not act, and cannot, out of a regard for the general welfare. In any economy, our natural indolence and selfishness require incentives. Some few persons always will act out of altruism; but they will not be numerous enough to sustain a modern economy, once the old incentives of advancement, profit, and acquisition of property are gone. This sad truth already has flashed upon the minds of the more serious socialists in England, dismayed at the flaws in their own creation, and has led to ominous talk among them of "new incentives"—"the stick as well as the carrot."

For the conserving of freedom of any sort, then, the economy must be free in considerable measure. I repeat that much of the popular discussion of economic questions is obsolete, because it is founded, especially in America, upon the assumption that we still are living in a nineteenth-century condition characterized by the pressure of population upon food supply. But the real problems of the twentieth century are different from those of the nineteenth century, often, especially in the economic sphere, and are in some respects more difficult to approach. Our conservative task is to reconcile personal freedom with the claims of modern technology, and to try to humanize an age in which Things are in the saddle.

The triumph of technology, though it has solved for the time being, here in America, the ancient problem of material want, has created new problems. But we need not march on, as if propelled by some ineluctable destiny, toward a complete collectivization of economic life, the exploded ideal of the nineteenth-century socialists. We can no longer afford to bow before ideology. Thinking is a painful process; but only by thought can ideology be kept in check; no ideologue ever was beaten on his own ground, except by another ideologue. It is vain to appeal to a theoretical "freedom" of the nineteenth century. It is worse than vain to suppose that, by simply repeating the words "freedom," "democracy," and "progress," we can reconcile a system of impersonal economic consolidation with the ancient personal liberties of our civilization. The person whom Mr. Sidney Hook calls the "ritualistic liberal" seems to think that all we have to do to keep our freedom is to complain constantly and irresponsibly that our freedom is being lost. Yet many of these same ritualistic liberals applaud the very economic and social processes that are reducing the domain of freedom. I hope that conservatives will do something more than this.

We cannot afford merely to drift with the current of events, applying the pragmatic solution of considering every case simply upon its own passing merits. Present policies tend directly toward the establishment of an economic collectivism, under one name or another, inimical to the Republic.

Certain measures of taxation, for instance, most conspicuous in Britain but differing only in degree in America, operate to destroy private enterprise in the old sense, to abolish the inheritance of property and the sense of responsibility that accompanies inheritance, and to substitute, in the long run, state compulsion for the ancient motives to integrity.

Little serious thought seems to be given to the consequences, for one thing, of continuing inheritance-taxes at their present rate; yet they now constitute confiscation, and are a levy upon capital, not a voluntary contribution out of income toward the maintenance of the Republic. A society so rich as ours can afford to tolerate rich men and women—and can afford to encourage, indeed, the bequest and inheritance of large properties. No social institution does more to develop decent leadership and a sense of responsibility than does the inheritance of large properties, and of the duties that accompany those properties. Tocqueville, observing a century and a quarter ago the American hostility toward inherited wealth, remarked that great fortunes confer benefits of many sorts upon the whole of society—in leadership, in the encouragement of the arts, in the support of letters, in the nurture of novel undertakings; while a multitude of petty competences, rags to riches and back to rags in one generation, encourages only arrogance and the expenditure of wealth in evanescent display and creature-comforts. I am not suggesting that the remedy for all our ills lies in repealing the inheritance-tax; I am merely saying that we need to think through such problems as this afresh, and to do our thinking free from the slogans of the ideologues.

And, if inherited wealth brings some measure of responsibility to a commonwealth, so do the old disciplines of thrift, self-advancement, and personal ownership. Some of the more intelligent Americans, in every class and occupation, now are aware of the menace of irresponsibility in economic life, which soon communicates itself to political life: the irresponsibility of the salaried managers of vast corporations, the irresponsibility of civil servants vested with brief authority upon which there is small check, the irresponsibility of labor-union officials who may have risen to high place principally through the arts of the demagogue. A Republic does not endure forever upon the moral and social capital of an earlier time. A sense of responsibility is produced by hard lessons, by private risk and accountability, by a humane education, by religious principle, by inherited rights and duties. A Republic whose leaders are the flies of a summer cannot expect to obtain ordinary integrity without the old motives to integrity; it will turn, in desperation, to the hero-administrator, the misty figure somewhere at the summit—and, in the end, that hero administrator no longer will be found.

It is not only the process of economic consolidation and the operation of positive law that diminish the sense of responsibility guarding ordered freedom in the Republic. Other measures, more technological than directly political, operate to make man into a machine-server, with a great deal of idleness but little true leisure, free in the sense that no one oppresses him directly, but servile in the sense that he has been deprived of the old interests and hopes in life: failing to come to man's estate, he remains a perpetual child. In our present equilibrium, here in America, we may seem to have given a large measure of economic prosperity to the mass of men and women, at small cost in freedom. But I am thinking of what this Republic, and all the world, may be fifty years from now.

Not being high-school debaters, conservatives do not possess facile and simple solutions to all these discontents. They merely say that the first step toward curing a malady is to diagnose the disease correctly. I suggest that we must find our happiness in work, or not at all; and that servile work, however economically profitable, is irreconcilable with social freedom. With John Henry Newman, in his reply to Sir Robert Peel more than a century gone, I am not offering any new ideology; I am merely appealing to those principles of morals and politics which have been known to mankind for a great while. "I am proposing no measures, but exposing a fallacy, and resisting a pretense. Let Benthamism reign, if men have no aspirations; but do not tell them to be romantic, and then solace them with glory."

Freedom, after all, is a romantic aspiration, earnestly desired by only a minority of men and women. (Romantic aspirations, I may add, are what make life worth living.) Only a small minority, too, feel clearly the call of responsibility. But, that freedom and that responsibility gone, the habitual freedom and the security of the great mass of men and women must slip away, also, in the economic sphere as in the political. There are some among us who do not desire to be solaced with the glories of *Brave New World*. Political economy had its beginnings in the work of philosophers who, whatever their deficiencies, were concerned primarily with the extension of freedom. Political economy is far gone in decay when it becomes no better than an apology for the reduction of men and women to a condition of prosperous servility.

The success of the American Republic, and the preservation of our old liberties, have been achieved in considerable part by our aversion, here in America, to divorcing theory from prudence. No other society ever had problems so complex as ours; but no society before our age ever had such a wealth of learning available, and such an economic margin, to aid in the solving of problems. The analysis of the real meaning of freedom, and the examination of the nature of responsibility, are available to us Americans at the slight cost of a little of our idle time. Yet many of us seem to prefer to wander, thoughtless, into a devil's sabbath of whirling machinery, presided over by the commissar.

Liberals and radicals offer us no solution to our grand difficulties; they either are content to drift with the current of events, or urge us actually to row faster down the stream which they call Progress, but which the conservative knows to be Decadence. The liberals and the radicals have forgotten the meaning of the Republic. But conservatives, who were not born yesterday, know that men and women have free will. A Republic dies only when its citizens have neglected the wisdom of their ancestors and the methods of right reason. There are more conservatives left among us than there were good men left in Sodom; and I think that, God willing, the conservatives will yet prevail.

One of the most eloquent of American conservative thinkers was a woman, Agnes Repplier. Miss Repplier was not inclined to exchange the reality of the American Republic for some utopia of the collectivists. Loving her country, she wrote, "If patriotism becomes an emotion too expansively benevolent to make men willing to live and die for something concrete like a king or a country, we shall have nothing left to fall back upon but sexual love, which is a strong individual urge, but lacks breadth and scope of purpose. It burned Troy; but it did not build Rome, or secure the Magna Carta, or frame the Constitution of the United States." Love of the Republic shelters all our other loves. That love is worth some sacrifice.

Index

A

Acton, Lord, 63

Adams, John, 1, 10, 17, 47, 55, 64, 82

Alfred, King, 15

Aristotle, 39, 44

B

Babbitt, Irving, 31

Bell, Bernard Iddings, 75, 87

Bentham, Jeremy, 17

Bierce, Ambrose, 81

Brameld, Theodore, 74

Brownson, Orestes, 10, 12, 40, 50

Burke, Edmund, ix, xi, 1-2, 4, 10, 33, 82-83, 86

C

Calhoun, John C., 10, 47, 91

Chesterton, G. K., 4, 15

Cicero, 82, 93

Coleridge, S. T., 83

Conant, James, 77

Condorcet, Marquis de, 47

D

Dewey, John, 74-75, 77

F

Falkland, Lord, 6

Freud, Sigmund, 18

G

Godwin, William, 25

H

Hamilton, Alexander, 1

Hartz, Louis, 48

Hearnshaw, F. J. C., 82

Hegel, W. F., 27

Hitler, Adolph, 40, 68
Hodgskin, Thomas, 25-26
Hofstadter, Richard, 48
Hogg, Quintin. *See* Hailsham
Hook, Sidney, 9

J
Jay, John, 47
Jefferson, Thomas, 45

L
Lincoln, Abraham, x, 10

M
Madison, James, 1, 10, 47
Maine, Sir Henry, 46, 56
Marx, Karl, 7, 18
Mill, John Stuart, 81
More, Paul Elmer, 57

N
Newman, John Henry, Cardinal, 101
Nisbet, R. A., xi, 34
Nock, Albert Jay, 42

O
Ortega y Gasset, Jose, 72
Orwell, George, 35, 66-67

P
Peel, Sir Robert, 101
Percy of Newcastle, Lord, 12

Proudhon, P.J., 55

R
Randolph of Roanoke, John, 10, 86
Repplier, Agnes, 102
Riesman, David, 79
Roosevelt, Franklin D., 53
Rossiter, Clinton, 48
Rousseau, J.-J., 50, 55
Ruskin, John, 60

S
Santayana, George, xi
Shaw, George Bernard, xii, 95
Sorokin, Pitirim, 36-38
Spencer, Herbert, 25

T
Tocqueville, Alexis de, 3, 39, 85, 99
Toynbee, Arnold, 12
Trollope, Anthony, 81

V
Voegelin, Eric, xi, 12

W
Whitehead, Alfred North, 76